Thatcher

FOR BEGINNERS

Peter Pugh and Carl Flint

Edited by Richard Appignanesi

ICON BOOKS

Published in 1997 by Icon Books Ltd.,
Grange Road, Duxford, Cambridge CB2 4QF

Distributed in the UK, Europe, Canada, South Africa and Asia
by the Penguin Group:
Penguin Books Ltd., 27 Wrights Lane, London W8 5TZ

Published in Australia in 1997 by Allen & Unwin Pty. Ltd.,
PO Box 8500, 9 Atchison Street, St. Leonards, NSW 2065

Originating editor: Richard Appignanesi

ISBN 1 874166 53 6

Printed and bound in Great Britain by
Biddles Ltd., Guildford and King's Lynn

Britain Before Thatcher

In February 1974 the Conservative Party, led by **Edward Heath** (b. 1916), was defeated in a General Election which had been precipitated by the government's failure to cope with the trades unions, most especially the National Union of Mineworkers. **Keith Joseph** (1918–96), a member of Heath's cabinet, attributed Britain's ills to the harmful effects of socialism:

> WE ARE NOW MORE SOCIALIST IN MANY WAYS THAN ANY OTHER DEVELOPED COUNTRY OUTSIDE THE COMMUNIST BLOC, IN THE SIZE OF THE PUBLIC SECTOR, THE RANGE OF CONTROLS AND THE TELESCOPING OF NET INCOME.

He went further, saying that Tory governments had travelled this path as surely and enthusiastically as Labour ones.

Was Joseph right? Was Britain **socialist** in the 1970s, and if so, how did it get that way?

Brief History of Post-War Britain

The Labour Party had grown in the first half of the 20th century into a mass party, and had won a decisive victory in the General Election at the end of the Second World War. The Election was held in early July 1945 when the Allies had achieved victory over Hitler in Europe but were still at war with Japan. Conservative Prime Minister **Winston Churchill** (1874–1965) came back from the peace negotiations in Potsdam with his deputy, Labour leader **Clement Attlee** (1883–1967), for the announcement of the results on 25 July 1945.

Furthermore, the Labour victory was overwhelming. They captured 393 seats in the House of Commons to the Conservatives' 189.

Some were surprised that the war leader and hero, Churchill, should be booted out, but others who had followed the findings of *Mass Observation*, had listened to the ordinary voter and seen the reaction to the *Beveridge Report*, were not.

They wanted what **Sir William Beveridge** (1879–1963), director of labour exchanges 1909–16 and a director of the London School of Economics 1919–37, had suggested in his report to the House of Commons in 1942. What was the *Beveridge Report*?

The Beveridge Report

Social insurance should be part of a general policy of social progress. Social security can only be achieved through co-operation between the individual and the state.

Special benefits should be provided for unusual expenses in connection with birth, marriage and death.

Pensions should be available for all.

There should be a free medical service.

The Welfare State

The *Report* was universally acclaimed.

The Labour Party elected in 1945 on a wave of enthusiasm for collective security and the effectiveness of planning – after all, the War had been won by **planning**, hadn't it? – legislated in its administration up to 1950 to bring in what became known as *The Welfare State*.

The nationalization of the means of production, distribution and exchange – the famous *Clause 4* of the Labour Party constitution – was tackled with vigour and enthusiasm by the incoming Labour administration.

Nationalization and Social Security

The following nationalizations took place under the new Labour government:

1946   Bank of England
1946   British Overseas Airways, British European Airways and British
        South American Airways
1946   Inland Transport Act (everything that ran on wheels for profit,
        except short-distance road haulage, lorries used by companies
        for their own products, and municipal bus companies)
1947   The Coal Industry
1948   Electricity
1948   Cable and Wireless
1948   Gas
1949   Steel

And, towering above all, the National Health Services Act (1946), providing "free" health care for all, described even by the Conservative MP, Derick Heathcoat-Amory (later Chancellor of the Exchequer) as: "By any test, a tremendous measure."

Keynesianism

The intellectual justification for this planned approach to the economy came from **John Maynard Keynes** (1883–1946).

OR RATHER FROM HOW MY WRITING WAS INTERPRETED.

Keynesianism required that the large institutions, corporations and unions should drive the country's economy and that the government should intervene constantly to balance the situation, increasing or decreasing financial stimuli where necessary.

THE LABOUR PARTY GREW OUT OF THE WORKING MAN'S DESIRE FOR MORE POLITICAL SAY.

AND OUR FIRST MEANS OF PROTECTION AGAINST THE CRUEL AND OPPRESSIVE EMPLOYERS OF LABOUR WAS THE TRADE UNION.

THE PARTY GREW FROM THE UNIONS, AND THE UNIONS WERE ALWAYS A SIGNIFICANT FORCE IN THE PARTY, ESPECIALLY AS UNION FUNDS FINANCED THE PARTY.

The Trade Union Movement

After a shaky start in the last decades of the 19th century, both the trade union movement and the Labour Party were given a great boost by the outrage in the working class following a court decision in 1901.

The first case was a great step forward for the unions and the Labour Party. The Act gave the unions formidable power to live outside the law, later to be greatly abused.

By 1945, the unions were a very powerful force within the labour movement and the Labour Party. **Denis Healey** (b. 1917), long-time Labour MP, Chancellor of the Exchequer and Foreign Secretary in Labour administrations, said in his autobiography, *The Time of My Life* . . .

Who Rules?

But if the leaders of the unions could dominate the Executive of the
Labour Party, ironically they were not as powerful within their own unions.
Denis Healey again . . .

*The real power lies not in the union headquarters but with the local
shop stewards . . . Moreover, the TUC* [Trades Union Congress, i.e. all
the bosses of the unions] *has no real power over its constituent unions,
unlike its equivalents in Scandinavia, Germany and Austria; in those
countries, governments have normally been able to rely on the annual
agreements made at national level between centralized organizations
of unions and employers, without direct government intervention. This
is even more true of Japan, where the recognized need for a national
consensus on all major economic issues has made possible 40 years
of high growth, full employment, rapidly rising living standards and
exceptionally low inflation.*

"Butskellism", or Consensus Politics

Appeasement of the unions was not the prerogative of the Labour Party – the Conservatives indulged in it too. Indeed, there was little to choose between the two parties' approach to economic and social issues for the first 30 years after the War. *The Economist* coined the word "Butskellism" – after the Tory Home Secretary, **Rab Butler** (1902–82) and the Labour leader, **Hugh Gaitskell** (1906–63) – to show how little difference there was in the two parties' approach.

BUTSKELLISM IS A TWO-PARTY CONSENSUS ABOUT . . .

the Welfare State

a mixed economy

full employment

consultation with the unions

in foreign policy – commitment to NATO (North Atlantic Treaty Organization), the nuclear deterrent, the run-down of Empire and the promotion of the Commonwealth

13

Caution and Restraint

The Conservative administrations of the 1950s which replaced the Labour administrations of 1945–50 and 1950–51 may have talked of a "bonfire of controls", but in 1960 government expenditure was a higher proportion of GNP (gross national product) at 41% than it had been in 1950 at 39%.

The Conservative Party's conscience about the working class was summed up by **Harold Macmillan** (1894–1986), Prime Minister from 1957–63.

Butskellism prevailed through all of the post-War governments, no matter the majority of the governing party, as shown below.

July 1945 – February 1950	Labour	204	majority
February 1950 – October 1951	Labour	17	
October 1951 – May 1955	Conservative	74	
May 1955 – May 1959	Conservative	57	
May 1959 – October 1964	Conservative	107	
October 1964 – April 1966	Labour	13	
April 1966 – June 1970	Labour	110	
June 1970 – February 1974	Conservative	43	

VOTE BUTSKELLISM

THIS ONLY CHANGED WHEN I WAS ELECTED TO THE LEADERSHIP OF THE CONSERVATIVE PARTY IN FEBRUARY 1975.

What's Wrong With Britain?

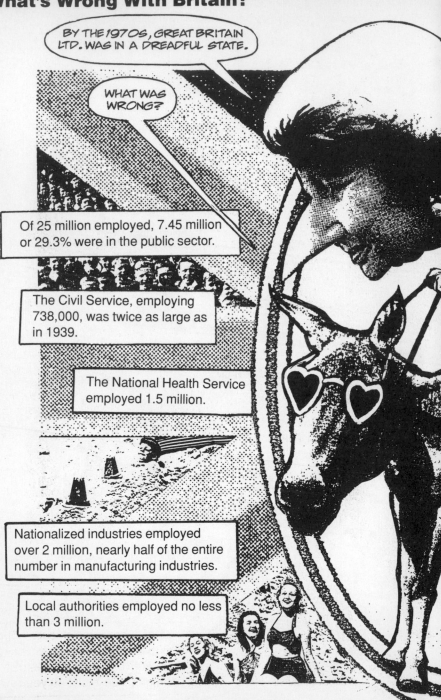

BY THE 1970S, GREAT BRITAIN LTD. WAS IN A DREADFUL STATE.

WHAT WAS WRONG?

Of 25 million employed, 7.45 million or 29.3% were in the public sector.

The Civil Service, employing 738,000, was twice as large as in 1939.

The National Health Service employed 1.5 million.

Nationalized industries employed over 2 million, nearly half of the entire number in manufacturing industries.

Local authorities employed no less than 3 million.

The subsidies (£4.6 billion) and borrowing (£2.5 billion) of the nationalized industries in 1979 were almost equal to the cost of servicing the national debt (£8.4 billion).

These subsidies were not going to growing industries such as electricity, whose supply had grown tenfold since 1938, but to old, declining industries such as coal, whose output had declined by a third, and rail, with half the miles of service as in 1938.

National per capita income – 40% above the West European average in the late 1950s – was below average by 1979.

Britain had the lowest growth of productivity of any major industrial economy, with an eight-fold increase in strikes compared with the 1930s.

The currency was declining fast, with the £ worth one twentieth of its 1938 value.

A loaf of bread which cost 1.5p in 1938 cost 65p in 1979, an increase of 4,200% in the most basic of commodities in just 40 years.

There had been the occasional attempt to stand out against the Keynesian approach. For example, Chancellor of the Exchequer **Peter Thorneycroft** (b. 1909) and two ministers at the Treasury, **Enoch Powell** (b. 1912) and **Nigel Birch** (1906–81) . . .

WE RESIGNED FROM THE CONSERVATIVE GOVERNMENT IN JANUARY 1958 OVER MACMILLAN'S REFUSAL TO ACCEPT OUR PROPOSED MONETARIST CUTS IN PUBLIC EXPENDITURE.

Labour Prime Minister **Harold Wilson** (1916–95) tried to bring the unions under some control with the help of **Barbara Castle** (b. 1910), Minister for Employment and Productivity.

WE INTRODUCED A WHITE PAPER, *IN PLACE OF STRIFE*, IN 1969.

When the unions protested, they backed down, setting the scene for the 1970s, a decade when government policy often seemed to be determined in TUC Congress House.

By the time **James Callaghan** (b. 1912) came to the end of his reign as Labour Prime Minister in 1979, cabinet papers were being sent to the TUC for approval. Callaghan said to the TUC General Council at 10 Downing Street . . .

The Rise of Heath

The Tories' long spell in power, later to be dubbed "13 years of Tory misrule", came to an end in October 1964 when the Labour Party under Harold Wilson, promising his "white-hot technological revolution", defeated them. Labour's majority was wafer-thin but in 1966 they improved it to around 100 and the Tories concentrated on re-thinking their policies for the future.

Traditionally, the leader of the Tory Party had been appointed by the grandees of the party after some consultation with other senior MPs.

Sir Alec Douglas-Home (1903–96) emerged as a compromise leader after an unpleasant series of squabbles and lobbying when Harold Macmillan resigned in 1963.

WHEN DOUGLAS-HOME STOOD DOWN AFTER HIS DEFEAT BY WILSON IN *1964*, THE FIRST ELECTION BROUGHT FORWARD AN UNTYPICAL TORY LEADER . . .

I INSTITUTED A MODERN ELECTION PROCESS.

EDWARD HEATH, THE SON OF A CARPENTER FROM BROADSTAIRS, KENT.

During the Tories' period in opposition in the second half of the 1960s, Heath started to shape his ideas, some of which challenged the consensus of the immediate post-War years. Heath talked of curbing the unions, the importance of competition, the need to reshape the welfare state with more emphasis on selectivity, and giving priority to business. Indeed, he told the Tory Party Conference after his Election victory in 1970 . . .

The End of "Selsdon Man"

However, the realities of government brought a series of U-turns, though in fact Heath had always believed in the necessity of the state being closely involved in the running of the economy. There had been much talk of allowing lame-duck companies to collapse, but in 1971 the government rescued first Rolls Royce, who had seriously underpriced their world-beating aircraft engine, the RB211, and then Upper Clyde Shipbuilders, whose outdated management and labour practices had made the company hopelessly uncompetitive.

The good resolutions of 1970 epitomized in "Selsdon Man" (after a Tory planning meeting at the Selsdon Park Hotel) went by the board. In February 1974, Heath was defeated in a General Election called to ask the country . . .

The National Union of Mineworkers had called a strike in the middle of a fuel crisis caused by a massive price rise and rationing by OPEC (Organization of Petroleum-Exporting Countries) in the winter of 1973–4.

Heath was defeated again in October 1974 when Labour tried to increase its majority, opening the way for a challenge to his leadership.

The ineffectiveness of the recently-enacted Industrial Relations Bill added to the general disillusionment.

Downslide and Paranoia

In 1973, **Lord Rothschild** (1910–90), head of the Central Policy Review staff (the civil service think-tank set up by Heath), said . . .

From the vantage point of the Cabinet Office it seems to me that unless we take a very strong pull at ourselves and give up the idea that we are one of the wealthiest, most influential and important countries of the world – in other words that Queen Victoria is still reigning – we are likely to find ourselves in increasingly serious trouble. To give just one unpalatable example, in 1985 we shall have half the economic weight of France or Germany.

As if to prove his prophecy correct, the International Monetary Fund (IMF) arrived to "look at the books" in 1976 before agreeing a loan, something that usually only happened to Third World countries.

In 1988, the economic historian Andrew Gamble reminded everyone of the situation in the mid-1970s.

Events suggested that a major crisis of hegemony was unfolding. Elements of the Right began to question democracy and endorse violence. The emergence of vigilante organizations, the speculation about military coups, and the plotting of elements of the security services against the Labour government were signs of the deep disorientation and profound demoralization which events in the early 1970s had created in sections of the British Establishment.

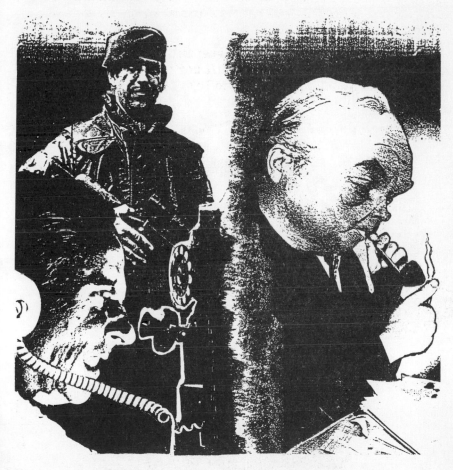

Such conditions made the time ripe for the Conservatives to elect a new leader.

The Intellectual Roots of Thatcherism

Margaret Thatcher once described **Friedrich von Hayek** (1899–1992) as one of the great intellects of the 20th century. There is no doubt that his book, *The Road to Serfdom*, published in London in 1944, was a seminal work which provided the philosophical basis of a free and competitive economy. Thatcher, irritated by some "wet" Conservative arguing for the "middle way", is reported to have pulled Hayek's *The Constitution of Liberty* from her briefcase, held it up for all to see and banged it down on the table.

Hayek was born in Vienna in 1899 into a minor aristocratic and strongly academic family. Ludwig Wittgenstein was a cousin and, like him, Hayek served in the Austrian army in the First World War. At the University of Vienna in the early 1920s he studied philosophy and economics and expounded mildly socialist views. One of his teachers was **Ludwig von Mises** (1881–1973), an outstanding developer of the Austrian school of economics.

MISES WAS *THE* RADICAL FREE MARKET ECONOMIST AND HIS *SOCIALISM*, PUBLISHED IN *1922*, CONVINCED ME OF THE INEFFICIENCY OF CENTRALIZED CONTROL AND TURNED ME INTO A CLASSIC LIBERAL.

Hayek and Mises saw society's function as encouraging individual activity and protecting diversity. This was in sharp contrast to the socialists who felt society should be fundamentally concerned with shepherding or persuading people towards achieving the common good. Hayek concluded that liberty under a minimalist state was the ideal.

A Free Market Philosophy

Hayek's writing provided Keith Joseph and Margaret Thatcher with the philosophical justification for what they said to the British public.

FALSE MONETARY AND CREDIT POLICY, PURSUED THROUGH ALMOST THE WHOLE PERIOD SINCE THE LAST WAR, HAS PLACED THE ECONOMIC SYSTEMS OF ALL THE WESTERN INDUSTRIAL COUNTRIES IN A HIGHLY UNSTABLE POSITION.

THE ARGUMENT OFTEN ADVANCED THAT INFLATION PRODUCES MERELY A REDISTRIBUTION OF THE SOCIAL PRODUCT, WHILE UNEMPLOYMENT REDUCES IT AND THEREFORE REPRESENTS A WORSE EVIL, IS THUS FALSE, BECAUSE INFLATION BECOMES THE CAUSE OF INCREASED UNEMPLOYMENT.

Free Market Democracy

In Britain in the 1970s, as the trade union barons held the country to ransom, Joseph and Thatcher did not need to look further than Hayek to show people what was happening: *For progress towards its aims, socialism needs government with unlimited powers . . . In such a system various groups must be given, not what a majority thinks they deserve, but what these groups think they are entitled to.*

By this Hayek meant that people should be paid what others are willing to pay for their services and it is wrong for society to try to put a value on those services. It is likely that this purely economic argument led Thatcher, towards the end of her period in office, to make a remark that probably did her more harm than almost any other.

THERE IS NO "VALUE TO SOCIETY".

THERE IS NO SUCH THING AS SOCIETY.

Social Justice

Hayek was also critical of "social justice".

When government interference is demanded in the name of social justice this now means, more often than not, the demand for the protection of the existing relative position of some group. "Social justice" has thus become little more than a demand for the protection of vested interests and the creation of new privilege, such as when in the name of social justice the farmer is assured "parity" with the industrial worker.

Individualism and Equality

When we turn to equality, it should be said at once that true individualism is not equalitarian in the modern sense of the word. It can see no reason for trying to make men equal as distinct from treating them equally. While individualism is profoundly opposed to all prescriptive privilege, to all protection, by law or force, of any rights not based on rules equally applicable to all persons, it also denies government the right to limit what the able or fortunate may achieve.

AN ECONOMIC SYSTEM IN WHICH EACH GETS WHAT OTHERS THINK HE DESERVES WOULD NECESSARILY BE A HIGHLY INEFFICIENT SYSTEM - QUITE APART FROM ITS BEING ALSO AN INTOLERABLY OPPRESSIVE SYSTEM.

Privatization

In his criticism of state monopolies, Hayek was providing the philosophical justification for the eventual Thatcher privatization programme.

Thatcherites also found support for their determination to reduce the monopolistic power of the trades unions: *The monopolistic practices which threaten the functioning of the market are today much more serious on the side of labour than on the side of enterprise, and the preservation of the market order will depend much more than on anything else, on whether we succeed in curbing the former.*

The Institute of Economic Affairs

Hayek's teaching and that of **Milton Friedman** (b. 1912) – especially his book, *Free to Choose*, whose main thesis propounded that when the free market is allowed to operate with the least interference from government the result is a highly desirable combination of economic progress and political freedom – found expression through the Institute of Economic Affairs (IEA).

The IEA was founded by a businessman, **Antony Fisher**, in 1957. Fisher had been greatly influenced by his reading a précis of Hayek's *The Road to Serfdom* in, of all things, *Reader's Digest*, in 1944. He sought out Hayek at the London School of Economics.

In the 1950s Fisher's Buxted Chicken Company became very successful, providing him with the money to set up the IEA, an organization to convert intellectual opinion exemplified by teachers, academics, students and leading journalists. **Ralph** (now **Lord**) **Harris** (b. 1924) became the IEA's first director general, moderating Fisher's original idea.

In 1959, a Liberal Party supporter, **Arthur Seldon** (b. 1916), became editorial director. Born in the East End of London, he lost both parents before he was three. Nevertheless he went on to win a scholarship to the London School of Economics, and became a dedicated supporter of the virtues of market capitalism and an opponent of socialism and collectivism.

In his book *Capitalism* (1990), Seldon attacked the collective consensus which he felt had operated in Britain since 1939.

Joseph and the IEA

The IEA was initially ignored by all politicians except Keith Joseph. He began to read its publications after 1964 and to discuss the economic theory with Harris and Seldon, and in 1974 he received a course in IEA classical liberalism.

Alfred Sherman (b. 1919), who, as we shall see, played a major role in the development of Joseph's thinking at this time, said of the IEA: *Had it not been for the IEA there would have been no Thatcher revolution. They prepared the ground. They were the John the Baptist of the 1950s and 1960s – pace Enoch Powell – the voice crying in the wilderness.*

The IEA's work was complemented by that of the Adam Smith Institute, named after one of the founding fathers of classical economic liberalism, **Adam Smith** (1723–90), whom many Thatcherites regarded as the founder of their beliefs.

Enoch Powell

At the same time, Enoch Powell was extolling to the Tory Party the value of the capitalist free economy which both Hayek and the IEA were advocating. Only that could make sure that "men shall be free to make their own choices, right or wrong, wise or foolish, to obey their own consciences, to follow their own initiatives".

HE ATTACKED SOCIALISTS AND THEIR PLANNING.

A LITTLE GROUP OF FALLIBLE MEN IN WHITEHALL, MAKING GUESSES ABOUT THE FUTURE, INFLUENCED BY POLITICAL PRESSURES AND PARTISAN PREJUDICES AND WORKING ON PROJECTIONS DRAWN FROM THE PAST BY A STAFF OF ECONOMISTS.

Powell wanted the flexibility of the market, "the ceaseless revision to which firms and industries and individuals are all the time subjecting their plans and their intentions. Thus change comes naturally, quietly and swiftly, before the economists have got around to noticing."

He was deeply critical of Heath and his method of trying to curb inflation by controlling wages and prices. These were merely the symptoms of inflation. The cause was the printing of money.

While Thatcher and her close supporters acknowledged their debt to Powell privately, senior Conservative **Ian Gow** (1937–90) said openly: *I probably have every one of his speeches on my bookshelves. I studied them. It was his influence, his very clear, very great lucidity. What he was saying long before 1974 is said by everybody now. He was a monetarist, right back.*

And it was Keith Joseph who provided the link between Hayek, Powell and the IEA to Thatcher's thinking, largely through the Centre for Policy Studies (CPS).

The Centre for Policy Studies

The CPS was the idea of Alfred Sherman, a Jew brought up in Hackney in the East End of London. With a Labour councillor father, Sherman was initially a socialist and joined the International Brigade, serving in Spain as a machine-gunner. When he returned to England in 1938 he was a Marxist. After the War he went to the London School of Economics and graduated into journalism.

I GRADUALLY BECAME DISILLUSIONED WITH COMMUNISM, EVEN WITH MILDER SOCIALISM, AND CAME TO SEE THE CONSERVATIVE PARTY AS THE ONLY POSSIBLE INSTRUMENT FOR ECONOMIC REFORM.

YOU KNOW WHO WAS CENTRAL TO ME? ALFRED SHERMAN. HE WAS VERY IMPORTANT.

Sherman was the man of energy who spurred the somewhat cerebral Joseph into action. It was Sherman who gave Keith Joseph the idea of a think-tank, independent of the Conservative Party and privately funded.

Joseph became the first chairman of the CPS, Sherman its director of studies. Thatcher and **Geoffrey Howe** (b. 1926) became directors, as well as **Nigel** (later **Lord**) **Vinson** (b. 1931), a successful businessman who had built up his own company before selling it in the 1960s. Sherman said of the CPS: *We started out to change the Conservative Party's approach; hence our primary aim was not to wean socialists away from socialism but to wean Conservatives away from the corporate state and Keynesian panaceas, which had helped bring about the Heath debacle . . . Our second major aim was trade-union reform.*

Thatcher's Roots

We must always remember that Thatcher was an *elected* leader. Furthermore, she was *not* of the Establishment. She saw her roots amongst the middle class, if not indeed the lower middle class.

As **Lord Blake** (b. 1916), the leading Conservative historian, said in 1989: *I don't think it's the world of White's, Pratt's and Brook's* [leading social clubs] *that she feels let down by, but the world of the Athenaeum* [élite academic, senior profession and ecclesiastical] *and the Reform* [media, politics and civil service]; *that's the Great and the Good. I think she does feel that a lot of the Great and the Good have let the country down. It is not accidental that she's never appointed a Royal Commission.*

Upbringing

Margaret Hilda Roberts was born on 13 October 1925, the younger daughter of Alderman Alfred Roberts (1893–1969) and Beatrice Roberts (d. 1960). She was to say later, "I owe almost everything to my father". Indeed her mother, who was a practical but passive housewife, was even excluded from Margaret Thatcher's *Who's Who* entry. When this was pointed out to her by a *Radio Times* interviewer in 1993, she became flustered.

Alfred Roberts was a self-made man. The son of a Northamptonshire shoemaker, he left school at 13 and went into the grocery business. In his early twenties he married and opened his own shop on the corner of the main London–Edinburgh road and the road to Nottingham, in a small sleepy town in the middle of England, Grantham.

BOTH OF MY DAUGHTERS WERE BORN ABOVE THE SHOP AND WERE BROUGHT UP STRICTLY TO BELIEVE IN HARD WORK, SELF-HELP, RIGOROUS BUDGETING AND THE IMPORTANCE OF SAVING.

Margaret said in a speech in 1982 . . .

"Some say I preach merely the homilies of housekeeping or the parables of the parlour. But I do not repent. Those parables would have saved many a financier from failure and many a country from crisis."

Alfred, though ill-educated himself, held a great respect for the benefits of education and was determined that Margaret, whom he saw as the brighter of his two daughters, should have the best education he could organize. There were piano lessons, compulsory library visits and attendance at an elementary school at the smarter end of town where Margaret was remembered as a questioning, eager pupil with a bulging satchel. She told the *Daily Telegraph* in 1980 . . .

Another dominant influence was Methodism. On Sundays, no newspapers were allowed and there were two visits to the Methodist church where Alfred preached.

Alfred also set the example of public service. He was a local councillor and became mayor in 1945. He was a governor of Kesteven and Grantham Girls' School, and later chairman. He was also a Justice of the Peace.

At school Margaret was hard-working, and although well-behaved and quiet she would always have a question for a visiting speaker. Her final report said: *Margaret is ambitious and deserves to do well.*

In 1943 she won a place at Somerville College, Oxford, where she read chemistry. She continued to be hard-working and efficient and, although not considered brilliant, was selected as an assistant by Professor Dorothy Hodgkin, who later won a Nobel Prize.

While at Oxford, her interest in politics was already surfacing, and she joined the Conservative Association. In the 1945 General Election she canvassed for **Quintin Hogg** (b. 1907).

Her tutor at Somerville, Janet Vaughan, said: *She was to me extremely interesting because she was a Conservative. The young at that time, especially at Somerville, were all pretty left-wing. She wasn't an interesting person except as a Conservative. If I had interesting, amusing people staying with me, I would never have thought of asking Margaret Roberts, except as a Conservative.*

When Margaret left Oxford in 1946 she used her chemistry degree to secure a job as a research chemist at British Xylonite Plastics in Manningtree, testing plastics for spectacle frames. After a year she moved to a J. Lyons factory in Hammersmith, testing the quality of cake fillings and ice cream. But this was just earning a living.

POLITICS WAS MY PASSION, AND IN THE 1950 ELECTION I STOOD AS THE CONSERVATIVE CANDIDATE FOR DARTFORD IN KENT.

She was faced with a 20,000 Labour majority and lost. At the next Election in 1951 she stood and lost again.

At this point her political career could have foundered, but she had met a local businessman, **Denis Thatcher** (b. 1915), and after her second defeat at the polls he asked her to marry him. They were married in December 1951. Later Margaret admitted the debt she owed to Denis, telling *The Guardian* in 1962: "I do not need to worry about money."

Margaret began to read for the Bar and passed her exams in December 1953. Thereafter she practised tax law on and off for five years. She told the *Sunday Graphic* in February 1952 that married women should be able to have careers: "In this way, gifts and talents that would otherwise be wasted are developed to the benefit of the community."

Commenting on the fact that there were only 17 women among the 625 MPs, she said . . .

Denis' money allowed Margaret to pursue her political career single-mindedly. She gave birth to twins, Mark and Carol, in 1953.

BUT A LIVE-IN NANNY WAS EMPLOYED TO LOOK AFTER THEM.

Her relationship with the children was not close, although Mark stands accused of financially exploiting his relationship to her once she became Prime Minister. Carol wrote a book about her father in 1996, *Below the Parapet*, and made one or two references to her mother's lack of interest.

SHE WAS PRONE TO CALLING ME BY HER SECRETARIES' NAMES AND WORKING THROUGH EACH OF THEM UNTIL SHE GOT TO CAROL.

Becoming an MP

Her frustration in the 1950s was not finding a Parliamentary seat. She tried for adoption in Orpington for a by-election but was rejected. Beckenham, Maidstone and Oxford all turned her down, but finally in 1958 her luck changed. Finchley in North London became vacant.

There were 200 applicants. She was short-listed, and against three middle-of-the-road typical Tory MP types, she won on the second ballot.

At the next General Election in 1959 she increased her majority to 16,260. Ironically, it was the Election when Prime Minister Harold Macmillan made his famous remark: *Let's be frank about it, most of our people have never had it so good.*

It was the high-tide of Conservative post-War consensualism and Thatcher was later to deride it for its lax fiscal discipline and feebleness in controlling public spending. Harold Wilson, leader of the Labour Party after Gaitskell, described Britain in the early 1960s as a "candy-floss society".

But Thatcher could not be worrying about the macro picture. At this point she had to make her mark as an ordinary MP. She made a strong and well-received maiden speech.

UNUSUALLY, IT WAS ATTACHED TO A PRIVATE MEMBER'S BILL WHOSE PURPOSE WAS TO GIVE THE PRESS RIGHTS OF ACCESS TO MEETINGS OF LOCAL COUNCILS.

Her mistrust of local government, so apparent when she became Prime Minister, went back a long way.

Her abilities were soon noted and she was appointed Parliamentary Secretary to the Ministry of Pensions. Three years' conscientious work there added a dislike of civil servants to her mistrust of local government.

A New Leader in 1975

The most obvious candidate from the right wing of the Tory Party was Keith Joseph, but he killed his chances with one passage from a speech he made to Birmingham Conservatives in which he expressed his concern at the quality of the population.

TOO MANY BABIES WERE BEING BORN TO PEOPLE AT THE BOTTOM END OF THE SOCIAL SCALE.

There was an immediate outcry and Joseph withdrew. Thatcher put her name forward. All the other heavyweight candidates were constrained by their loyalty to Heath. Furthermore, this relatively unknown woman was unwittingly helped by Heath himself.

I MADE HER NUMBER TWO SHADOW SPOKESPERSON ON TREASURY AFFAIRS.

AND I MADE EVERY USE OF MY POSITION TO GOAD CHANCELLOR OF THE EXCHEQUER DENIS HEALEY INTO DIGNIFYING ME BY CALLING ME . . .

THE PASIONARA OF PRIVILEGE!

Thatcher's campaign was masterminded by the scheming **Airey Neave** (1916–79). There could be no better plotter than this ex-POW who had himself escaped from Colditz Castle in the War and then organized other escape routes across Europe. Before the vote he whispered to Labour minister, **Roy Hattersley** (b. 1932) . . .

MY FILLY IS GOING TO WIN.

AND HE WAS RIGHT. THE RESULTS OF THE FIRST BALLOT SHOWED IT.

Margaret Thatcher	130
Edward Heath	119
Hugh Fraser	16

This result was not enough for an outright win but it knocked out Heath and left the way open for the Tory heavyweights to enter the ring. However, Thatcher's momentum was now unstoppable and the results of the second ballot were:

Margaret Thatcher	146
Willie Whitelaw	79
Geoffrey Howe	19
James Prior	19
John Peyton	11

The Tory Party had a new leader. Life would never be the same again.

Who Helped Thatcher to Power?

It is easy to fall into the trap of thinking that Thatcher always dominated the Tory Party from the moment she was elected leader. By the mid-1980s she certainly did dominate it. But in 1975 she did not.

SHE WAS USED AS A MEANS OF GETTING RID OF HEATH - AND WE DIDN'T HAVE ANYBODY ELSE.

Even *The Economist*, later to become a strong supporter of Thatcher, declared itself for Heath before the leadership election. She herself knew that her challenge was a tremendous gamble.

I KNOW THAT IF I LOSE, MY POLITICAL CAREER IS OVER.

Questions were raised about the desirability of having for leader a Grantham grocer's daughter with a second-class degree in Chemistry, who was only in politics because of a rich husband.

Thatcher's Early Allies

Thatcher needed allies. Her first three were: **Willie Whitelaw** (b. 1918)

> I HAD INSTANTLY DECLARED MY LOYALTY AFTER MY DEFEAT IN THE LEADERSHIP ELECTION.

Geoffrey Howe (b. 1926), who had become disillusioned with Heathism

> IN SPITE OF THE FACT OF BEING CLOSELY INVOLVED WITH DRAFTING HEATH'S INCOMES POLICY.

And **John Biffen** (b. 1930), long an enemy of Heath corporatism.

> I DESCRIBED HEATH AS A GLORIFIED MANAGEMENT CONSULTANT.

At her first party conference in autumn 1975, Thatcher made her position clear.

Britain and socialism are not the same thing, and as long as I have health and strength they never will be . . . Let me give you my vision: a man's right to work as he will, to spend what he earns, to own property, to have the state as servant and not as master; these are the British inheritance. They are the essence of a free country, and on that freedom all other freedoms depend.

In the background, Keith Joseph was making speeches propounding the view that government could not create jobs, should not intervene on incomes and could not act in the public interest by increasing demand.

In 1977 the party produced a pamphlet, *The Right Approach to the Economy*. It was largely the work of Joseph, Howe, **David Howell** (b. 1936), a strong Thatcher supporter, and **Jim Prior** (b. 1927), who could be considered a Tory who still favoured "the middle way".

Interestingly, privatization was hardly mentioned, and there was not a single commitment to hostile measures against the trade unions.

Thatcherites in the Late 1970s

As well as Joseph and Sherman, others now began to line up behind Thatcher, urging a new approach.

John (now **Sir John**) **Hoskyns** (b. 1927), a handsome, articulate businessman, had joined the army after Winchester, and then IBM. He had set up his own computer business and sold it in 1975. He saw business as the agent of economic recovery and initially did not care which party he supported as long as they would listen to him. However, his dislike of trade unions led him inevitably to the Tories and, as the unions behaved in a more and more autocratic fashion in the late 1970s, he made it his job to turn them into a liability for the Labour Party. He determined to "drag every skeleton out of the union cupboard, linking it with Labour".

Hoskyns put it in down-to-earth terms.

By the early 1970s it was quite clear . . . that the UK really was going down. I spent a lot of my time in the USA on business and I began to realize what a scruffy, second-rate little economy we were. And there were Americans who were beginning to say, "We're worried that we're going the same way as you are!".

Inventing the Thatcher Image

Gordon Reece (b. 1930), a producer of TV light entertainment programmes, soon gained "an apparently unassailable place in Mrs T's affections" and the *Sunday Times* said of him: *She likes him and admires him and so she's going to look after him* . . .

HE MAKES ME LAUGH, I LIKE THAT.

He was the forerunner of what came to be seen as the Thatcherite stereotype. A natty dresser, charming and a bit flash, he smoked big cigars and drank only champagne. His father, a car salesman from Liverpool, had sent him to a minor Roman Catholic public school, Ratcliffe. In 1979 he separated from his wife and six children and moved between hotels and the houses of friends.

Reece took it on himself to school Thatcher in her TV presentation, advising her to avoid fussy clothes, jewellery and plunging necklines.

I WANTED HER IN A TUNIC DRESS WITH A BLOUSE UNDERNEATH. I ALSO LOWERED HER SHRILL VOICE AND RE-SHAPED HER HAIR.

Reece introduced Thatcher to **Maurice Saatchi** (b. 1946) and **Charles Saatchi** (b. 1943), referred to by *Private Eye* as "the Corsican twins", who had set up their own very successful advertising agency.

WITH FRONT-MAN *TIM* (NOW *SIR TIM*) *BELL* (B. 1941) WE WERE GIVEN RESPONSIBILITY FOR PROJECTING A NEW IMAGE FOR THE TORY PARTY IN TIME FOR THE NEXT ELECTION.

Another active supporter of Thatcher during the opposition years was **Angus Maude** (b. 1912), who was chairman of the Conservative Research Department.

I DRAFTED MANY OF THE KEY PARTY PUBLICATIONS, INCLUDING *THE RIGHT APPROACH* (1976) AND *THE RIGHT APPROACH TO THE ECONOMY* (1977).

A Thatcherite almost before Thatcher, **Nicholas Ridley** (b. 1929) was the only minister to resign over Heath's U-turn.

I WAS A PIONEER OF PRIVATIZATION, SAYING OPENLY IN THE LATE 1970S THAT ALL THE NATIONALIZED INDUSTRIES WERE A DISGRACE.

Norman Strauss was another key planner in the development of Thatcherite plans in the late 1970s. He worked closely with Hoskyns to produce *Stepping Stones*, effectively the blueprint for Thatcher's first term, 1979–83.

Norman Tebbit (b. 1931) became the quintessential Thatcherite MP, happy to describe himself as "upwardly mobile". An early and vociferous supporter of Thatcher's leadership bid, he worked closely with Airey Neave on briefing Thatcher for Parliamentary Questions. He was well rewarded with government posts when Thatcher came to power, and helped give the Thatcher administrations a reputation for harshness with his comment at the 1981 Tory conference, as unemployment soared:

MY FATHER DID NOT WHINGE IN THE *1930S* BUT GOT ON HIS BIKE TO FIND WORK.

Supported passionately by this group, especially for the first ten to twelve years of her leadership, Thatcher was able to turn the Tory Party away from the British post-War consensus. She had learnt from reading Hayek and Friedman, but she did not make the mistake of turning them into party dogma. She wanted people to have a mood about Britain, not work from a set of texts. Sherman said: *It is very difficult to say Hayek was a guru for Keith and Margaret. I would say not. They turned to Hayek and Friedman to justify what they already thought.*

Early Champions of Monetarism

Alan Walters (b. 1926), whose father was a Communist, came from a working-class home in Leicester and served as a private during the Second World War. He had met Enoch Powell in the early 1950s and both became convinced that monetarist economics was important for Britain. Powell introduced Walters to both **Iain Macleod** (1926–70), who was to be Chancellor of the Exchequer very briefly in Heath's administration in 1970 before dying suddenly, and Keith Joseph. Walters was also in touch with the economists at the IEA. Convinced, after a spell as visiting professor of economics at Northwestern University in Evanston, Chicago, of the importance of the quantity of money in the economic system, he was shocked when he returned to Britain in 1959.

MOST CIVIL SERVANTS DID NOT KNOW WHAT I WAS TALKING ABOUT!

Furthermore, the *Radcliffe Report* on the monetary and credit system had just been published and said that the supply of money was of no interest to economic management. Walters said: "The view prevalent among British economists, and confirmed by the *Radcliffe Report* . . . was dangerously wrong."

Keith Joseph held discussions with Walters during the 1960s on monetarist theories and applications. He introduced Thatcher to him and the two politicians would go to Walters' apartment for tutorials in economics. Walters was to become totally disillusioned with Heath, especially after his U-turn, and with Wilson.

Walters left for the USA but kept in touch and, thanks to Sherman, returned to Britain when Thatcher was in power in 1980.

A slightly incongruous Thatcher supporter in the late 1970s was her speech writer, **Ronnie Millar** (b. 1919), odd because he had written speeches for Heath. When Thatcher arrived as leader in 1975 someone suggested him and she agreed to look at what he wrote. His first speech for her, on Conservative philosophy, ended with an Abraham Lincoln quote.

YOU CANNOT ENRICH THE POOR BY IMPOVERISHING THE RICH. YOU CANNOT STRENGTHEN THE WEAK BY WEAKENING THE STRONG.

Thatcher read it, put it down, scrabbled in her handbag and pulled out a scrap of paper which quoted the same words!

AFTER THAT, MILLAR COULD DO NO WRONG.

In Power – May 1979

The have-plentys and want-mores were eager for Thatcher, while the have-nots, have-littles and have-problems were not so sure. In the end, the timing of the Election, fatally delayed by Callaghan from the autumn of 1978, gave the unions the whole winter to break his pay policy and cause absolute havoc. The Tories gained 69 more seats than Labour and an overall majority of 41.

What had Thatcher promised?

Heath's government had come to power with well-researched and detailed plans, but when they were subjected to the multifarious pressures of office they displayed rigidity and broke, and Heath reverted to "incomes policy, lavish industrial support and eventual coalition centrism". (*The Economist*, April 1979)

Nevertheless, certain promises had been made and Thatcher was determined to keep them.

The cutting of personal taxation.

The reduction of public expenditure.

The curbing of trade union power.

And she had, as Ferdinand Mount wrote in the *Spectator*: . . . *said it again . . . and again, and again . . . she stands for less government and lower taxes and for people standing on their own two feet . . . Whether Margaret Thatcher succeeds or fails as Prime Minister, there can be no doubt that as leader of the opposition she has gingered up the argument.*

Before looking at the effects of Thatcherism on British institutions, we must have some chronology of the Thatcher years in power, highlighting the main events.

Thatcher came to power at a singularly unpropitious moment economically. On the international scene, the world was still recovering from the recession caused by the quintupling of oil prices in 1973/4.

Domestically, Thatcher had made a mistake in promising to honour the inflationary pay awards suggested by the Clegg Commission.

The Clegg Commission had been set up by the Labour government in response to the public sector strikes in "the winter of discontent", 1978–9. As Hugo Young said in his book, *One of Us*:

Clegg produced a formula of great extravagance. It eventually led to a 25% increase in the public sector wage bill over 12 months. It said nothing about waste, nothing about manning and was, in effect, an incomes policy which did not even have the merit of restraining pay.

However, Thatcher, desperate for power and fearful of alienating public sector voters, agreed to honour it.

The British economy was where Thatcher wanted to concentrate her efforts.

Another "overseas" problem was Europe, but at least this was related to the economy.

BUT I WAS FORCED TO SPEND A GREAT DEAL OF MY TIME TRYING TO FINALIZE A REASONABLE SETTLEMENT OF THE RHODESIA PROBLEM.

AND I COULD HAMMER AWAY AT THE EUROPEAN HEADS OF STATE ABOUT BRITAIN'S "EXCESSIVE" CONTRIBUTIONS.

As the problems of the British economy proved even more intractable than she expected, it suited her to blame the Europeans for taking "our" money.

But in her first administration the major issue was the British economy. As the world slid into another recession, Britain's structural weaknesses – reliance on smoke-stack industries, overmanning, poor productivity, weak management and intransigent unions – were cruelly exposed. Even the one piece of good fortune – North Sea Oil, by this time in full flow – proved harmful in the sense that it helped drive the £ higher and higher, thereby intensifying the squeeze on British manufacturers. Some felt that Thatcher and one or two others in her government were not unhappy about a high exchange rate facilitating the closure of obsolete smoke-stack industries.

"The Lady's Not For Turning"

1980 was a very difficult year. Manufacturing output fell sharply and
unemployment rose by 836,000 (more than any year since the 1930s).
Between July 1979 and July 1980, prices rose by 22%, wages by 20%.
As the monetarist approach, so long and determinedly advocated by the
Thatcherites in opposition, was clearly not working and was apparently
destroying not only the worst but also some of the better British
manufacturers, morale plunged in the ranks of the government. However,
one person remained obdurate and, with the help of her speech-writer,
Ronnie Millar, came up with a memorable line at the 1980 Conservative
Party conference where everyone was talking of the inevitable U-turn:

* Reference to a play by Christopher Fry,
The Lady's Not For Burning (1948).

72

In the spring of 1981, with unemployment at 2.7 million and still rising and output down 5.5% in two years, there was enormous pressure for the Budget to reduce the squeeze on spending and taxes. Most in the Treasury and even supposed monetarists like the Chancellor, Geoffrey Howe, favoured a little relaxation.

The result was a budget which, to the incredulity of many, increased taxes further and reduced public spending. With hindsight the Thatcherites claimed it as the budget which laid the foundation for the successful growth of the 1980s.

Battling the Unions

The other great battle of Thatcher's first administration was with the unions. Her government faced down a number of major strikes, including a national steel strike in 1980.

Although in this case, the employers did raise their offer from 2% to 16%...

But Thatcher gradually got the message over. These were different days from the 1970s when "beer and sandwiches" with the union leaders at No. 10 was the prelude to another abject government surrender. Thatcher did occasionally meet union leaders if she couldn't avoid it, but she treated them with contempt, saying in the Commons . . .

All of this strife meant that by the end of 1981 the opinion polls were giving the Tories a very low rating but, significantly, also showed Thatcher to be the most unpopular Prime Minister (only a 23% approval) since polling began.

The Falklands Rescue

As dreadful 1981 turned into dismal 1982, an event took place which had everyone scrambling for their atlases. Argentina grew impatient with the British Foreign Office's ambiguous signals over their future intentions towards the Falkland Islands (the Malvinas to the Argentinians), and invaded them.

Thatcher could be accused of negligence before the event. Once it had occurred, transformed into Warrior Queen, she gave it her undivided attention until she emerged victorious two months later with 255 British and 650 Argentinian dead. Allied to her victories over the unions and the "wets" in her cabinet, it made her position unassailable and guaranteed her another term in office. By June 1982 her approval rating had soared from the 23% in December to 51%.

The jingoists loved it – winning wars again, the British have always been good at that. The more thoughtful wondered why the whole affair was not referred to the United Nations. Others were sickened by the triumphalist tone of the celebrations over the victory.

But many Thatcherites were less than impressed when Archbishop Runcie at the victory thanksgiving service in St Paul's Cathedral remembered the Argentinian as well as the British mourners.

The Second Administration, 1983–7

The dominant theme of Thatcher's second administration was again the economy. By this time, it presented a happier picture, with unemployment stabilizing and then falling, inflation staying under control, output rising and productivity improving. Whereas her first administration had been hampered by a sharp rise in the price of oil, her second was aided by a sharp decline.

Immediately after the Election in June 1983 she carried out a major cabinet reshuffle, in which the most significant change was the replacement of Geoffrey Howe with **Nigel Lawson** (b. 1932) as Chancellor.

He was also Chancellor during the period when one of Thatcherism's more enduring legacies, privatization (again, more later), moved to "full ahead".

Tackling the Unions Again

The great battle of Thatcher's second administration was with the National Union of Mineworkers. The defeat of the Callaghan Labour government in May 1979 which brought Thatcher to power was arguably the fourth time since the War that the unions had contributed significantly to the loss of power by the incumbent government. In 1951, their hostility to Clement Attlee's policies was a factor in his defeat, and certainly their resistance to Wilson's attempt to curb their abuse of power in 1969 helped destabilize his government, ousted by Heath in 1970. Most famous of all, the unions led by the miners were a significant factor in Heath's defeat in the February 1974 Election. Ironically, three of these defeats were suffered by the Labour Party, the supposed champions of the unions. Furthermore, the defeat of Heath ushered in Margaret Thatcher, who became determined to curb their powers once and for all.

In tackling union power, Thatcher was faced with a slight dilemma.

I HAD ADOPTED THE MILTON FRIEDMAN VIEW THAT INFLATION WAS NOT CAUSED BY UNIONS BUT BY THE PRINTING OF TOO MUCH MONEY.

NEVERTHELESS, WE THATCHERITES SEE UNIONS AS INEFFICIENT, ABUSIVE, RESTRICTIVE LEECHES ON THE SIDE OF BRITISH MANUFACTURERS.

AND UNLESS THEY'RE BROUGHT TO BOOK, BRITISH COMPANIES WILL NOT BE ABLE TO THRIVE IN THE NEW, LIBERAL, LOW-INFLATION ENVIRONMENT WE'RE DETERMINED TO CREATE.

As we have seen, plenty of people saw the unions as a significant factor in Britain's relative economic decline. Hayek for one.

The trade unions have become the biggest obstacle to raising the living standards of the working class as a whole; they are the chief cause of unemployment and the main reason for the decline of the British economy . . . Britain remains paralysed by the consequences of the coercive powers irresponsibly conferred on the unions by law; there can be no salvation for her until these special privileges are revoked. *

* From a series of essays published by the IEA, *Unemployment and the Unions: The Distortion of Relative Prices by Monopoly in the Labour Market*

How to Curb the Unions

Thatcher was nothing if not a politician and she knew how previous attempts to bring the unions back into the framework of the law had foundered. She proceeded cautiously, and indeed her first Secretary of State for Employment, Jim Prior, was an old Heathite who believed strongly in the powers of conciliation and gentle persuasion.

It removed the immunity of union officials and members from legal action by an employer not party to the dispute, but left the immunity of the union as such intact. It made secondary picketing unlawful.

Inevitably there was a great outcry from the unions, and even the employers felt it would do little to curb the unions' abuses of their bargaining powers.

Others felt the Act did not go far enough. Thatcher agreed with this view, despatched Prior to Northern Ireland and replaced him with the more abrasive Norman Tebbit, one of her "trusties". The second Act in October 1982 tackled union immunity from liability for damages for unlawful actions.

Even Tebbit did not face removing immunity from strikes carried out without a secret ballot.

Tebbit's successor, **Tom King** (b. 1933), brought in the Trade Union Act of 1984 which introduced secret ballots for union elections, political activities and strikes.

IN *1985*, I STRETCHED FROM ONE YEAR TO TWO THE PERIOD AFTER WHICH AN EMPLOYEE COULD CLAIM UNFAIR DIS-MISSAL UNDER LABOUR'S EMPLOYMENT PROTECTION ACT *1975*.

Lord Young (b. 1932), succeeding King in 1985, concerned himself more with the freeing up of the supply side of the labour market, and in the Sex Discrimination Act of 1986 derestricted women's hours.

MINIMUM WAGES SET BY WAGES COUNCILS WHICH COVERED OVER A TENTH OF THE LABOUR FORCE WERE ABOLISHED FOR UNDER-21S IN THE *1986* WAGES ACT.

IT ALSO TIGHTENED UP THE RULES ON SECRET BALLOTS AND THE USE OF UNION FUNDS.

IN THE *1988* EMPLOYMENT ACT, STATUTORY SUPPORT FOR THE CLOSED SHOP WAS REMOVED AND EMPLOYEES PROTECTED AGAINST DIS-MISSAL FOR NON-UNION MEMBERSHIP.

The 1989 Act removed restrictions on the use of women for certain types of work and on young people's hours of work. The 1990 Act strengthened the law against dismissal for non-union membership and also strengthened the employers' position in dismissal for unofficial industrial action.

The Miners' Strike, 1984

The biggest union confrontation of the Thatcher years was the year-long strike of the miners in 1984. Ever the pragmatist, Thatcher had backed away from confrontation in 1981 when advised that coal stocks were not high enough. After that, Thatcher made sure that stocks at the power stations were built up and when **Arthur Scargill** (b. 1938), the President of the National Union of Mineworkers, called his men out without a ballot in the spring of 1984, Thatcher was ready.

The scene was set for an epic battle.

Profile of Arthur Scargill

Arthur Scargill had fought his way to the top of the Yorkshire coal miners' union, making his mark as a young, militant, articulate member in sharp contrast to the older, more conservative delegates on the executive committee. As one miner pointed out, he was the first member of the committee for a long time who didn't have soup stains on his waistcoat.

He became President of the Yorkshire Miners and the obvious successor to Joe Gormley as President of the National Union of Mineworkers (NUM) when he retired in 1981.

The scene for the battle was set immediately after the Conservative Election victory, when Scargill made an inflammatory speech likening the Conservatives to the Nazis in Germany in the 1930s. *A fight against this government's policies will inevitably take place outside rather than inside Parliament . . . I am not prepared to accept policies proposed by a government elected by a minority of the British electorate . . . Extra-parliamentary action will be the only course open to the working class and the Labour movement.*

On 1 March 1984, the National Coal Board (NCB) announced the intended closure of one of its uneconomic pits, Cortonwood. Scargill immediately called a strike – without a ballot – and on 12 March the strike began. Many in the Nottinghamshire pits were reluctant to strike, and the local union organized a ballot. The result was 73% against a strike. Scargill dealt with this insubordination by sending in masses of flying pickets. Violence escalated through April and May up to a massive confrontation at the Orgreave Coke Works, where 5,000 pickets fought a pitched battle with police.

Throughout the summer of 1984, fortunes ebbed and flowed.

Talks collapsed on 18 July and Thatcher, who felt that a resounding and clear-cut victory was necessary, recalled in her autobiography: *I have to say that I was enormously relieved. It was crucial for the future of the industry and for the future of the country itself that the NUM's claim that uneconomic pits should never be closed should be defeated, and be seen to be defeated, and the use of strikes for political purposes discredited once and for all.*

The big threat for the government and hope for the miners was that the National Association of Colliery Overmen, Deputies and Shotfirers (NACODS) would call a strike of their own. If they did, every pit would have to shut on safety grounds. They had, in fact, voted to strike in April 1984, but with less than the necessary two thirds majority. However, in August 1984 the NCB made a near-fatal mistake by threatening to withhold the pay of NACODS members who refused to cross NUM picket lines. On 28 September NACODS held another ballot and this time 82.5% voted in favour of a strike.

The NUM Defeated

However, October was to bring a series of hammer blows to Scargill and the NUM. On 10 October, the legislation that the Conservatives had introduced began to bear fruit when fines of £1,000 and £200,000 were imposed on Scargill and the NUM respectively for contempt of court.

In April 1984 a British policewoman, PC Fletcher, had been killed in St James's Square by a gunshot from the Libyan embassy, and association with such a régime did not win the miners any friends.

The NCB followed this up by encouraging a gradual return to work, offering to pay the usual Christmas bonus to all those at work by 19 November. The following week 2,203 returned, in spite of the threats and violence. And in case anyone was in doubt about the level of violence, at the end of November a lump of concrete was hurled from a bridge, killing a taxi-driver carrying a miner to work.

In late December, the chairman of the Electricity Board was able to announce that they would get through the winter without any power cuts. By mid-January 1985 there were more than 75,000 miners back at work. On 27 February, more than half the miners were back, and on 3 March the NUM executive committee voted to call off the strike.

The "enemy within", as Thatcher referred to Scargill (General Galtieri in the Falklands War had been the "enemy without"), had been defeated. A key element in the battle had been the creation of a central police co-ordination authority which could mobilize police forces from all over the country. This last was crucial in preventing the mass picketing from intimidating the government as it had in the miners' strikes during Heath's administration in the 1970s.

It was estimated that the cost of the strike to the economy was £2 billion and extra public expenditure was £300 million. However, Chancellor of the Exchequer Nigel Lawson, irritated though he was by this expenditure, said he regarded it as "even in narrow financial terms . . . a worthwhile investment for the nation".

And Lawson was right.

The 1984 Act made the secret ballot a legal requirement (1) for the election of voting members to the executive council of the unions at intervals not greater than five years; (2) for all those who might be called on to take official industrial action; and (3) for setting up or retaining an existing political fund.

Scargill, with his ranting and bullying tactics, proved to be the Tories' greatest friend. If he hadn't existed they would have had to invent him.

Murdoch vs. the Printers' Union

Another significant strike occurred at the new offices of News International when it moved from strike-torn Fleet Street to Wapping in early 1986. Again, massive police presence was required to protect non-printing union workers who operated the plant. These were members of the Electricians' union who had struck a deal with **Rupert Murdoch** (b. 1931), a tough Australian businessman greatly admired by Thatcher.

Union practices in Fleet Street had long been a scandal and were highlighted by the journalist **Bernard Levin** (b. 1928) in an article in *The Times* in 1986.

Incredibly, the proprietors agreed, and so began what became known on Fleet Street as "fat" – payment for work not done. Levin wrote: *For many years now newspapers have been produced in conditions which combined a protection racket with a lunatic asylum; the details would have made interesting reading for those who bought the newspapers but any attempt to let the outside world know what was happening nightly would have led immediately to a strike.*

AT THE END OF THE 19TH CENTURY, THE SAME ADVERTISEMENT PLACED IN SEVERAL NEWSPAPERS HAD TO BE COMPOSED EVERY TIME, OR IF NOT THE COMPOSITORS STILL HAD TO BE PAID FOR DOING NOTHING.

WITH THE SUPPORT OF NEW LAWS AND A DETERMINED GOVERNMENT, I PUT AN END TO ALL THAT!

The Thatcherite attempt to bring order to the unions was helped by other factors as well as new laws and the facing down of strikes. Partly due to the decline of manufacturing, union membership fell sharply. In 1979, membership was 13.3 million but by 1986 it was 10.5 million, and the decline continued, though at a slower rate.

Trade Union Membership and Stoppages

	Total membership		Working days lost through stoppages (per thousand employees)				
	(m)	(% of employees)	UK	USA	France	Italy	Australia
1979	13.3	57.4	1270	230	180	1920	780
1980	12.9	56.4	520	230	90	1140	630
1981	12.1	55.3	190	190	80	730	780
1982	11.6	54.2	250	100	130	1280	370
1983	11.2	53.4	180	190	70	980	310
1984	11.0	51.8	1280	90	70	610	240
1985	10.8	50.5	300	70	40	270	230
1986	10.5	49.3	90	120	30	390	240
1987	10.5	48.5	160	40	30	320	220

Also contributing to a less militant approach by unions has been the growth in unemployment. It rose to just over 1 million at the end of the Callaghan government in 1978, enabling the Saatchis to make a big impact with their advertisement showing a long dole queue and the slogan "Labour isn't working". However, under Thatcher's government, unemployment rose sharply to 3 million and did not start to fall until 1986. It then fell rapidly to under 2 million by 1990 but rose again to nearly 3 million by 1993.

Ben Roberts, Emeritus Professor of Industrial Relations at the London School of Economics, and the first President of the International Industrial Relations Association from 1965–73, said: *The reform of industrial relations and the results that have followed must rank as one of Mrs Thatcher's greatest achievements. Government policies . . . have resulted in a significant reduction in union power, which has brought considerable benefits to all sections of society.*

Enoch Powell, whom most Thatcherites admired, but who did not always feel the same about them, certainly admired Thatcher's tackling of the union problem.

Thatcher's bringing of order into union affairs also contributed to one of the unsung achievements of her era – the strong inward investments by overseas companies, especially from Japan, who came to see the country as an efficient producer and the ideal entry into the European market.

The Westland Affair

The closest that Thatcher came to being toppled in her long reign was in early 1986 when a cabinet argument over the fate of a small British helicopter manufacturer revealed deceptions at the highest levels of government. **Michael Heseltine** (b. 1933), never a Thatcher favourite, resigned over what he saw as Thatcher's dictatorial behaviour.

... THE EMERGENCE OF WHAT I CONSIDER TO BE THE BREAKDOWN OF CONSTITUTIONAL GOVERNMENT.

Thatcher herself admitted that the affair came close to forcing her resignation, as she left for question time in the House.

I MAY NOT BE PRIME MINISTER BY SIX O'CLOCK TONIGHT.

Fortunately for her, the relatively new Labour leader, **Neil Kinnock** (b. 1942), failed to stick to the point and ask the right questions. He blustered and she escaped.

Economic Success

The Westland affair shook the government and fascinated political watchers but the vast mass of the electorate were more interested in the mundane facts of life – jobs, money, inflation, law and order – and as 1986 unfolded the economic scene brightened. The price of oil fell and fell, and Nigel Lawson, spurning the opportunity to reduce inflation, made sure the £ fell with it and added fuel to an already growing economy. (Lawson could have held the £ up, making imports cheaper, which, along with a lower price for oil, would have reduced the rate of inflation.) In the four years after the 1983 Election, average weekly earnings rose by 15% in real terms. At last unemployment stopped rising and indeed began to fall quite sharply.

There were a few wobbles during the campaign but Thatcher was re-elected with another comfortable majority, again helped by a split opposition, although Labour under Neil and Glenys Kinnock were more credible than the party of Michael Foot in 1983.

Thatcherism in Practice

Education

It must have come as a surprise, and perhaps a hurtful one, that the hero of many Thatcherites, Enoch Powell, was scathing in his criticism of their approach to education: *The old Prussia claimed to decide how its citizens should be educated to make them efficient instruments of its imperialism. The new Prussia, now being daily built here, demands, after having substituted economic competition for military aggression, that its citizens be so educated as to maximize their return on the capital invested.*

More predictably, Martin Jacques, the editor of *Marxism Today*, said the Thatcher government regarded universities "with as much contempt as it does the trade unions . . . It is a know-nothing government whose philistinism is dangerous to the economic and cultural health of the nation."

Even the CPS, that great bastion of Thatcherism, came close to criticizing Thatcher's Education Act of 1988. In a pamphlet the CPS commissioned but refused to publish, Professor Elie Kedourie of the LSE attacked the government's assumptions that since universities are state-funded, they must serve the public interest; and that because ministers are the elected representatives of the taxpayers, they ought to lay down what the public interest requires universities to do. "This sweeping doctrine leans to the centralization which is the distinguishing feature of enlightened absolutism."

In their education policies, the Thatcherites had no Friedrich von Hayek, no Milton Friedman, no IEA to provide a thought-out policy. They knew they wanted to make Britain more efficient and therefore the education system, including the universities, should fit into that scheme.

From the very beginning, Thatcher made cuts in higher education. In 1981, universities were allowed one month to plan an 18% cut in budgets over 3 years. 3,000 posts were eliminated. Although the 1983 manifesto promised no more cuts, in 1984 further cuts of 2% were demanded.

One of the biggest indictments of the Thatcher years is the neglect of education and training. In December 1988, Charles Leadbeater made a damning comparison in the *Financial Times*. *In West Germany, 30% of school-leavers at 16 had an intermediate certificate based on an assessment of 10 subjects. Only 12% of British school-leavers reached a comparable level.*

The Civil Service

We have already seen that Thatcher's spell at the Ministry of Pensions had given her a deep antipathy towards the Civil Service – "Iron entered my soul". When she came to power, one of her first acts was to appoint **Sir Derek Rayner** (b. 1926), a director of Marks and Spencer, as an "efficiency auditor". He struggled with the usual Whitehall obfuscation and blocking techniques.

BUT I BACKED HIM AT EVERY TURN, AND HE SUCCEEDED IN MAKING SAVINGS BY THE MID-1980s OF £1 BILLION, THE EQUIVALENT OF 22 NEW HOSPITALS!

By 1987, the Civil Service had been cut back by some 20% to 600,000, the lowest level since the War, and its running costs were measurable and under control. Rayner's departmental management systems were acknowledged by permanent secretaries, in public and in private, as being valuable tools of management which should be retained whichever government was in power.

Rayner's successor, **Sir Robin Ibbs** (b. 1926) of ICI, continued the war on waste. By 1987, no less than 27,000 forms had been scrapped and another 41,000 redesigned. Furthermore, Ibbs produced a document, *The Next Steps*, which was radical in that it suggested that the majority of Civil Service activities should be seen for what they were, businesses delivering services to the public. After much wrangling between Whitehall and the Treasury, steps were taken to implement these proposals, and a series of agencies was set up to improve efficiency.

There were accusations of promotion to the very top of those who were "one of us". Pay parities were not maintained. Working conditions were not improved (Rayner, with his M & S background, was particularly unhappy about this). There was the feeling that Thatcher herself held civil servants responsible for Britain's decline under the influence of Beveridge and Keynes.

The Welfare State

The British public loves its welfare state, and it was Thatcher's constant criticism of it that brought her more unpopularity than almost anything else.

IN FACT MORE WAS SPENT ON WELFARE IN THE 1980S IN REAL TERMS THAN EVER BEFORE, BUT NO ONE BELIEVED IT.

At 1987/8 prices

Education: £17.46 billion was spent in 1988–9, compared with £15.9 billion in 1978–9.

Health: £20.5 billion was spent in 1988–9, compared with £15.2 billion in 1978–9.

Social Security: £44.8 billion was spent in 1988–9, compared with £33.7 billion in 1978–9.

In 1991, the London School of Economics showed in its publication, *The State of Welfare*, that expenditure on the welfare state was a third higher in real terms in 1987/8 than it had been in 1973/4.

In spite of these increases, people could see the Thatcherites itching to save money and reduce the "dependency" culture that had become so ingrained. In 1982, the Central Policy Review Staff suggested . . .

Private health insurance for all.

The removal of indexation from many benefits.

The ending of state funding of higher education.

What Thatcher did achieve was to subject the swollen welfare bureaucracy to more business-like management. Value-for-money and efficiency audits became commonplace. She insisted that even the grandest public sector employees, such as professors and hospital consultants, should account for their use of public funds. Thatcher talked tough, but she left Britain still more of a welfare state than an enterprise society.

The NHS

Thatcher's governments were nothing if not full of rhetoric on the need to rein back public expenditure, and the National Health Service was subjected to this rhetoric too.

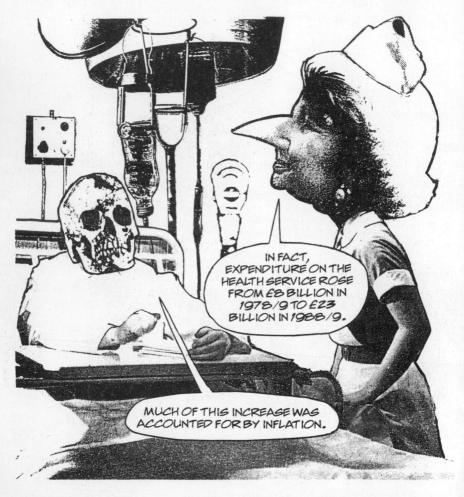

According to journalist Charles Webster: *Taking Mrs Thatcher's term of office as a whole, the average annual real rise in NHS expenditure on current goods and services is smaller than that of any previous administration. In fact it is only half the level of any administration since 1960 . . . Britain is now resolutely located at the foot of the league table of health expenditure of comparable Western nations.*

The Arts

Government support for the arts had grown steadily since the creation of the Arts Council in 1945, and had excited little comment until the Thatcherites viewed the subsidies as alien to their belief in self-help.

The movers and shakers in academia and the arts felt a particular loathing for Thatcher, both for what they saw as philistinism and for the fact that the comfortable days of unlimited funds were gone.

Europe

Thatcher herself had two major battles with the European Community, one at the beginning of her reign as Prime Minister and one at the end. In between was the long-running saga of whether Britain should join the Exchange Rate Mechanism (ERM) of the European Monetary System (EMS).

When she came to power in May 1979 her argument with the EC, or EEC as it was then called, was all about money.

> THE TREASURY CANNOT ESTABLISH EXACTLY WHAT IT FEELS THE *EEC* IS COSTING THE COUNTRY, BUT A FIGURE OF £1,000 MILLION HAS BEEN VIRTUALLY INVENTED.

> I SET OFF TO DEMAND THE RETURN OF "OUR MONEY" EVERYWHERE I WENT.

Finally, at a meeting of the European heads of state in Dublin in November 1979, she demanded the £1,000 million. **Christopher Tugendhat** (b. 1937), European Commissioner, wrote: *As the vehemence of her arguments increased, Schmidt* [German Chancellor] *at one point feigned sleep, and when she refused to give in, the French party's cars were drawn up outside with their engines running in order to emphasize the take-it-or-leave-it nature of their offer.*

Negotiations continued into 1980 and a compromise agreement was finally reached. Thatcher wanted to reject what was on offer from Europe, but for once her cabinet stood up to her. There were those who felt it suited her politically, as economic problems mounted at home, to be able to show the British public that she was standing up to these Europeans who were causing such hardship. Even **Roy Jenkins** (b. 1920), President of the European Commission at the time, said: *As a proponent of the British case, she does have the advantage of being almost totally impervious to how much she offends other people.*

As for **Ian Gilmour** (b. 1926), already disillusioned with Thatcher's economic policies, he now doubted her capacity for rational behaviour. His days in the cabinet were numbered!

Friendship With Reagan

For most of her time as Prime Minister, Thatcher's relations with the EC were lukewarm. Surprisingly, she established a much better relationship with the socialist French President **François Mitterrand** (1916–96) than she had ever achieved with the more right-wing **Valéry Giscard d'Estaing** (b. 1926), whom she described as not merely patrician but "Olympian". Nevertheless, Mitterrand said that she possessed "the eyes of Caligula and the mouth of Marilyn Monroe".

It was to the United States that she turned, forming a close relationship with President **Ronald Reagan** (b. 1911). Reagan had first met Thatcher on a visit to London in 1975 and the two became close personal allies. She was the first head of state to visit Reagan after his inauguration as President in January 1981. They agreed on foreign policy.

WHEN THE SOVIET UNION CALLED MAGGIE "THE IRON LADY", I RESPONDED BY CALLING THE SOVIET UNION "THE EVIL EMPIRE".

WE AGREED TOO ON THE ECONOMY, WITH "SETTING FREE", "SOUND MONEY" AND "DEREGULATION" CROPPING UP REGULARLY IN BOTH OUR SPEECHES.

In many ways their close friendship was surprising, because Reagan displayed all the characteristics most designed to irritate Thatcher. *Time* magazine criticized him for his intellectual passivity, unreflectiveness, lack of attachment to detail, obstinacy and detachment from reality. Even before important meetings, he rarely read briefing papers, and he shirked reaching difficult decisions.

The friendship was further cemented by the close support Britain received from its American ally in the Falklands War. **Sir Nicholas Henderson** (b. 1919), Britain's ambassador in Washington, said: *It is difficult to exaggerate the difference that America's support made to the military outcome.*

And the Atlantic Alliance prospered for the whole of the 1980s. In return for the help in the Falklands conflict, the US was allowed to use British bases to bomb Libya in early 1986. There was a slight hiccup when American troops invaded Grenada, a Commonwealth country, without warning Britain first, but this was a mere blip in an otherwise continuous period of mutual admiration. Throughout the decade, British ministers were despatched to the US to study initiatives for reviving inner cities, on health care, education and prisons. Furthermore, Thatcher, having supported the USA against the "evil empire", was one of the first to appreciate the significance of **Mikhail Gorbachev** (b. 1931), a man with whom she "could do business".

112

In contrast, Europe remained a vexed question, and by 1987 the Frenchman **Jacques Delors** (b. 1925), appointed President of the European Commission in 1985, was beginning to infuriate Thatcher, especially when he declared that Britain could afford to contribute more to the EC budget. In a speech to the European Parliament in Strasbourg in July 1988, Delors said that within ten years 80% of economic legislation, and possibly fiscal and social legislation also, would be of European rather than national origin. Thatcher was apoplectic.

WE HAVE NOT SUCCESSFULLY ROLLED BACK THE FRONTIERS OF THE STATE IN BRITAIN ONLY TO SEE THEM REIMPOSED AT A EUROPEAN LEVEL, WITH A EUROPEAN SUPER-STATE EXERCISING A NEW DOMINANCE FROM BRUSSELS.

And Delors did not endear himself to the Thatcher anti-federalists when he told the TUC . . .

YOU HAVE TOTALLY FAILED TO DEFEAT THE PRIME MINISTER IN THIS COUNTRY, BUT YOU HAVE AN OPPORTUNITY THROUGH BRUSSELS AND STRASBOURG TO BRING IN SOCIAL LEGISLATION WHICH WOULD BE HELPFUL TO YOUR CAUSE.

Thatcher retorted with a comment about "socialism by the back door" or "by the back Delors!".

The Speech at Bruges

By 1989, Thatcher's anti-European stance was beginning to upset erstwhile supporters. Ferdinand Mount wished she would see the Community as an opportunity rather than a threat.

What was the Thatcherite position on Europe?

Thatcher's speech at Bruges in 1988, one of the great set-pieces of her eleven-year reign, sets out what she and many of her closest supporters believed:

MY FIRST GUIDING PRINCIPLE IS THIS: WILLING AND ACTIVE CO-OPERATION BETWEEN INDEPENDENT SOVEREIGN STATES . . . EUROPE WILL BE STRONGER PRECISELY BECAUSE IT HAS FRANCE AS FRANCE, SPAIN AS SPAIN, BRITAIN AS BRITAIN, EACH WITH ITS OWN CUSTOMS, TRADITIONS AND IDENTITY. IT WOULD BE FOLLY TO TRY TO FIT THEM INTO SOME SORT OF IDENTIKIT EUROPEAN PERSONALITY.

But as well as "France as France" etc., there was an underswell of arrogance and xenophobia: *Britain is a home for people from the rest of Europe who sought sanctuary from tyranny.*

We British have in a special way contributed to Europe. Over the centuries we have fought to prevent Europe from falling under the dominance of a single power. We have fought and we have died for her freedom . . . throughout the last War kept alive the flame of liberty . . . From our island fortress the liberation of Europe itself was mounted.

Furthermore, the value of the Anglo-American alliance was emphasized: *Nor should we forget that European values have helped to make the United States of America into the valiant defender of freedom which she has become . . . People went there to get away from the intolerance and constraints of life in Europe.*

There was strong and implied criticism of Europe in the praise for the freedoms enjoyed by the British: *Britain has been in the lead in opening its markets to others, the City of London, our market for telecommunications, air transport, our coastal shipping trade, free movement of capital, a genuinely free market in financial services . . . I wish I could say the same of many other Community members.*

Privatization

Privatization became one of the most enduring of the Thatcher legacies, not only in Britain but in many countries throughout the world. However, it was not part of the Thatcherite vocabulary in the build-up to the 1979 Election. The manifesto promised only the sale back of the recently nationalized aerospace and shipbuilding companies, the selling of shares in the National Freight Corporation and the disposal of the National Enterprise Board's holdings.

It was Chancellor Nigel Lawson who gave the programme coherence after the 1983 Election.

BY THE END OF THE *1980s*, THE PRESUMPTION WAS THAT EVERY-THING THAT *COULD BE SOLD* **SHOULD** BE. THE MAIN MOTIVES WERE . . .

to reduce the role of the state in the economy and restore the powers of decision to the individual;

to implement the ideal of the property-owning democracy;

to improve productive efficiency;

to introduce allocative efficiency by substituting competitive free-market pricing for administered prices and controlled rents;

to finance the PSBR (Public Sector Borrowing Requirement) and reduce claims upon it;

to promote wide share ownership and subject management to more democratic control;

to encourage employee share ownership, thereby improving industrial relations.

The intellectual case against the nationalized industries had been set out by **John Redwood** (b. 1951), then a Fellow of All Souls, Oxford, later to become head of Mrs Thatcher's policy unit (and even later to challenge John Major for the leadership of the Tory Party) in an article in the *Lloyds Bank Review* in 1976.

The most famous criticism of the privatization programme came from Lord Stockton (formerly Harold Macmillan) when he described asset sales to finance current expenditure as . . .

IN MY VIEW, THEY MISALLOCATE CAPITAL, DISTORT DEMAND BY UNDER- OR OVER-PRICING, INFLATE MONEY SUPPLY THROUGH BORROWING, PAY INTEREST ON THEIR FUNDS AT BELOW MARKET RATES AND SUFFER POOR INDUSTRIAL RELATIONS.

SELLING THE FAMILY SILVER!

NO, IT'S SELLING IT BACK TO THE FAMILY.

There was not much point in holding on to the family silver anyway if it was losing you £30 a second, as the British Steel Corporation was in 1980. By 1989, British Steel was producing as much steel as in 1979 but with one third of the labour force.

Even the programme's greatest admirers would admit that some of the privatization sales were rushed through without sufficient attention to the original aim of broadening competition and protecting the interests of consumers.

There was no doubt who were the initial beneficiaries. Professor John Kay of the London Business School wrote: *Whatever the economic consequences of privatization, it has proved a highly remunerative activity for three groups: the initial shareholders, the managers (whose salaries have risen sharply), and the extensive group of professional advisers.*

Few could argue with the success in purely financial terms. British Telecom, British Steel, British Gas, British Airways and the British Airports Authority were by the early 1990s all hugely profitable companies in the private sector, whereas in the 1970s many of them had been drains on the Exchequer.

Individual Home and Share Ownership

By the 1990s no one expected, and very few desired, re-nationalization. The idea of the state running commercial enterprises was dead. Between 1977 and 1995 the British government raised $97 billion from privatization. Between 1996 and 2000, a leading merchant bank expected European governments to raise between $250 and $300 billion.

Thatcherites also believed in property ownership, and here they were certainly successful in pushing up owner-occupation to one of the highest levels in the industrial world.

Does It Benefit the Individual?

MP **Norman Lamont** (b. 1942), later Chancellor of the Exchequer under John Major, said in 1988: *If I had to choose a statistic that summed up the Thatcher years it is that. The number of people now owning shares is not much less than those who belong to trade unions.*

In fact shareholdings were not of great depth. Only 300,000 people owned a portfolio of over ten shares and only another 800,000 owned between four and nine. A Thatcher scheme to promote wider share ownership, Personal Equity Plans (PEPs), were used mainly by existing shareholders to take advantage of tax breaks.

INDEED, MOST STOCKBROKERS DON'T WANT SMALL SHAREHOLDERS BECAUSE THEY'RE NOT COST-EFFECTIVE.

In 1987, **Tony Blair** (b. 1953), then Labour's City spokesman, carried out a survey on selling 200 BT shares.

OF 151 STOCKBROKERS, ONE THIRD REFUSED TO DEAL, AND ANOTHER THIRD WOULD CHARGE A COMMISSION SO HIGH IT WIPED OUT ANY PROFIT. THE CITY IS "THE UNAPPROACHABLE FACE OF CAPITALISM".

Greed is Good

Kenneth Baker (b. 1934), Secretary of State for Education and Science in the late 1980s, preached social conscience and charity.

In 1995, the *Financial Times* said of the company Provident Financial, which specialized in lending to the poor at high rates of interest: *It is an unpalatable thought, but Provident Financial is benefiting from growing inequality in Britain. Economic stagnation in low-income areas and job insecurity are leaving more families unable to borrow money from traditional lenders such as banks, building societies and credit card providers. Provident exists to fill this gap.*

And fill it Provident did, making £101 million profit in 1995 and paying its directors total remuneration of £1.67 million. In spite of Baker's hopes, the company gave precisely **£51,000** to charity! As Gordon Gekko said in the film *Wall Street*, "Greed is good."

By the middle of Thatcher's reign the message had spread – it was OK to make money. In real life, the jailed Wall Street arbitrageur, **Ivan Boesky** (b. 1937), echoed Gekko's words.

A whole new breed grew up.

YUPPIES – Young upwardly mobile professionals

 or

YAPPIES – Young affluent professionals who tried to become respectable by turning into

GRUPPIES –   Green urban professionals

A New Breed – A New Language

New definitions of well-known words and phrases entered the language.

Asset stripper — nothing to do with night clubs, but financial operators who bought companies and sold off their assets, often making thousands redundant.

Blow his tits off — not sure quite what this meant before, but in Thatcher's world it meant "sell it to him". Its converse was "Ship it in shag".

Chartists — not forerunners of the unions, but those who predicted future share movements by past performance.

Chinese Walls — nothing to do with China, but supposed barriers within the new giant investment banks to prevent the stockbroking side buying shares just before the corporate side announced a takeover they were working on.

Churning — not your stomach after all the champagne, but the buying and selling of your client's shares for no better reason than it earned you commission.

Concert Party — correct, nothing to do with music, but the ganging up of predators before buying shares in a company.

Butterfly — only pretty in the sense that it's a no-lose situation in a traded option play.

Dog — obvious what a dog is, but in this case it's a share that has performed badly for years. Best example – Government War Loan.

Head and Shoulders — no, not a dandruff treatment but a share shout giving the signal, sell.

Stag — by the end of the Thatcher era at least nine million new shareholders knew what a stag was – a punter who applied for new issues with the sole intention of selling them instantly.

Streaker — plenty of those at Twickenham and Lords, but in Essex boy's language it's a zero coupon bond, i.e. one with no interest, issued at a deep discount to give, by the time of redemption, a computed interest rate at face value on maturity.

Being able to understand that made them worth their £250,000 a year, didn't it?

Thatcher's Children – or Orphans?

Some thought Thatcher's Britain a bleak world populated only by lonely buyers and sellers trying to do each other down. In 1989 the *Spectator* spoke of "bourgeois triumphalism", and the *Sunday Times* wrote "vulgarianism rules OK". Even the *Daily Telegraph* wailed that Britain had "ceased to be a nation of decency". The Governor of the Bank of England, **Robin Leigh-Pemberton** (b. 1927), told the *Sunday Times* in June 1990: *Old style thrift has gone out of fashion. The attitude is, "I want it and I want it now".*

Salman Rushdie (b. 1947) put it more crudely in *The Satanic Verses*.

The deputy leader of the Labour Party, Roy Hattersley, talked of Thatcher's children.

DELINQUENCY WAS THE BY-PRODUCT OF THEIR AFFLUENCE, COMBINED WITH THEIR REJECTION OF ANY SORT OF RESPONSIBILITY FOR THEIR NEIGHBOUR'S WELFARE . . . GREED AND INDIVIDUAL GAIN ARE THE GODS WHICH THEY ARE URGED TO WORSHIP.

It took one of Thatcher's own government, Kenneth Baker, the preacher of "charity", to articulate what many saw as the worst aspect of Thatcherism, in a speech to the Bow Group.

TORIES DO NOT NEED TO APOLOGIZE FOR THE INCREASED SCOPE WE HAVE GIVEN TO WHAT MIGHT BE CALLED ACQUISITIVE INDIVIDUALISM.

SOAP

And other members of Thatcher's cabinet began to express concern by the end of the 1980s. **Douglas Hurd** (b. 1930), after a visit to some market towns in middle England, said: *You do not find much poverty or social deprivation there. What you do find are too many young people with too much money in their pockets, too many pints inside them, but too little notion of the care and responsibility they owe to others.*

The strongly anglophile **Ralf Dahrendorf** (b. 1929), Warden of St Antony's College, Oxford, added: *There is now a widespread sense that a little more community is necessary – very hard to do by the same people who have first broken those institutions.*

127

The Poll Tax (1989)

Everyone was agreed that the **rates**, a local property-based tax stretching back nearly 100 years, was an unsatisfactory method of financing local government. Rates were based on the valuation of property. The value changed every so often, necessitating changes in rates, causing howls of rage from the losers. Thatcher objected to the rates for three reasons.

There seemed to be five alternatives.

1. Local sales tax

2. Local income tax

3. Revenues assigned by central to local government

4. Reform of the existing system

5. **A poll tax**

Thatcher was persuaded that a poll tax, or "community charge" as she insisted on calling it, was the answer.

A poll is a head and the tax was a **per head tax** on people. It was the poll tax.

A Big Mistake

David Butler (b. 1924), the psephologist of the age, analyzed the introduction of the tax in a book, *Failure in British Government: The Politics of the Poll Tax*. He showed how a group of officials and relatively junior ministers, determined to change the local tax system with a per capita charge, convinced Thatcher that they were right. Once convinced, Thatcher, an "elective dictatorship", was able to bulldoze the necessary legislation through, against the opposition of the Labour Party and the local authorities.

Thatcher had long held an aversion to the local rating system and, as Shadow Environment Secretary, got the commitment to abolish domestic rates into the Tory manifesto for the October 1974 Election. It stayed there in the 1979 manifesto.

Whatever the merits of the poll tax over the existing rating system, its implementation was a disaster. Common sense dictated a gradual phasing in, but Thatcher, on a high after her third victory in June 1987, combined with Nicholas Ridley to persuade a cabinet committee to go for the "Big Bang" approach.

Here's how Robert Harris described the poll tax fiasco in the *Sunday Times,* February 1991:

Even the right-wing *Economist* described the above as an under-statement, writing further: *The poll tax, alias the community charge, was the most misguided piece of domestic policy produced by any British government in this century. It was replaced within two years. It cost taxpayers not less than £1.5 billion. It cost Mrs Thatcher her job.*

Thatcher's Disregard of the Cabinet

The poll tax issue showed more clearly than any other how Thatcher dominated her cabinet. As her administrations progressed, fewer and fewer matters received thorough discussion in full cabinet. In her first government, she did not risk the cabinet scuppering what had already been decided. The Permanent Secretary, **Sir Douglas Wass** (b. 1923), said it in November 1979: *Do you know, there hasn't been a single economic discussion in the cabinet since this government came in?*

According to Nigel Lawson in his book *The View From Number 11,* the debate and decision over ERM membership never went to full cabinet. While Ian Gilmour, in *Dancing with Dogma,* maintained that Thatcher's decision to allow the US to use British bases for bombing Libya was made after consultation with just three ministers.

Thatcher's Downfall?

In the words of Douglas Hurd: *The main reason for Margaret Thatcher's loss of leadership was, I believe, her failure over the years to make the best of the cabinet system . . . She did not understand that colleagues too had knowledge and views and she relied on her individual powers excessively.*

The cabinet did not discuss the poll tax until January 1986, fifteen months after the initial studies team had been established, and seven months after the key decision in principle had been taken by a cabinet committee.

The answer was the size of the Tory majority in the House of Commons – over 100 – and probably a two-to-one Tory predominance in the House of Lords.

Black Monday

Thatcher's arrogance left her increasingly isolated. Whatever doubts about her position she may have felt in her first two governments, a third victory made her unassailable, and therein lay the seeds of her downfall. "We can do no wrong" is a fatal attitude and large mistakes were now made concerning Europe, the ERM and the poll tax (of which more later). The economic skies seemed blue when Thatcher was re-elected in June 1987.

In such situations the old enemy of stability, inflation, rears its ugly head.

With memories of the early 1920s and 1945–8, no country is more fearful of inflation than Germany. In the summer of 1987, the Bundesbank and the Federal Reserve Board in the US indulged in a public row over interest rates.

THE SPECTRE OF A DIFFERENT INTEREST–RATE CLIMATE JANGLED THE NERVES OF EQUITY HOLDERS, AND SUDDENLY STOCK MARKETS ROUND THE WORLD WENT CRASHING DOWN.

LED BY NEW YORK WHERE THE DOW JONES LOST NO LESS THAN 508 POINTS IN A SINGLE DAY, ALL THE MAJOR MARKETS FELL 25% IN TWO DAYS.

This all seemed to happen out of the blue, but stock markets usually foretell the truth, and indeed within eighteen months it was clear that many of the world's economies had been growing at an unsustainable rate and that a period of retrenchment was necessary.

Thatcher Resigns

For Britain, where inflation rose to double figures again by the end of 1990, it was back to good old-fashioned stop-go, or rather go-stop, a feature supposedly banished by all the supply-side reforms of the 1980s. Thatcher blamed her Chancellor, Lawson, who resigned in October 1989, ostensibly over interference by Alan Walters. Suddenly the Thatcherite miracle cures looked less miraculous. As rows over the poll tax and Europe broke out, Thatcher herself, seemingly impregnable after her third election victory, began to look vulnerable.

As the polls suggested that the Tories would not be re-elected with her as leader, the knives came out.

Thatcher was replaced not by Heseltine, but by the supposedly emollient **John Major** (b. 1943).

The Economic Results of Thatcherism

If Thatcher had retired in 1988, even in May 1989, ten years after she came to power, history would have judged the economic consequences of her administrations more favourably. By the time she resigned in November 1990, it was clear that the supposed Thatcher economic miracle of high growth and low inflation was less than miraculous.

Output
From peak to trough 1979 to 1981, manufacturing output fell by a staggering 15% and only strong growth in 1987 and 1988 took it above the 1979 level.

Inflation
The 12 month rate increased from 10.3% in May 1979 to an horrific 21.9% in August 1980, from where it fell sharply into single figures by 1982. From 1983 to 1988 it ranged between 3.5 and 6%, compared with 2 to 4.4% in other leading industrial countries. In 1990, inflation rose again to double figures in response to the domestic overheating of 1988/9.

Unemployment

The living standards of those in work rose more consistently than in any other decade of the century, but on the other hand unemployment rose sharply from 1.09 million in May 1979 to 2.13 million in May 1981, and went on rising to 3.13 million in July 1986. Thereafter it fell to 1.66 million in 1990 but, as recession struck again, rose to 2.9 million in 1993. Furthermore . . .

Taxes

The cutting of taxes was one of the main planks of Thatcherism. Indeed, in the first budget of June 1979, income tax was cut, and income tax rates, especially at the higher levels, were cut consistently through the 1980s.

top marginal rate was cut from 83 to 40%

basic rate was cut from 33 to 25%

tax allowances were raised by 25% in real terms

investment income surcharge of 15% was abolished

corporation tax was cut from 52 to 35%

capital transfer tax was simplified and top rate on inheritance tax reduced from 75 to 40%

capital gains tax was restructured to eliminate tax on inflationary gains

controls on prices, dividends, pay and foreign exchange were abolished

and so were restrictions on bank lending and hire purchase.

The new freedom given to the banks with regard to controls on their balance sheets was highly significant in creating the Thatcher Boom. Between 1980 and 1988 personal debt *doubled*.

However, other taxes were raised. VAT (value added tax) was almost doubled in 1979 from 8 to 15% and was raised further to 17.5% in 1991 to help finance the clearing up of the poll tax fiasco.

Employee national insurance contributions were also raised.

These tables taken from parliamentary reports in *Hansard*, 3 April 1990, allow for no doubt as to who were the major beneficiaries of Thatcher's tax policies.

Gains from income-tax and NIC charges, 1978–79 to 1990–91

	Married man, multiples of average earnings				
	2/3	1	2	5	10
Tax + NIC % of gross earnings					
1978–79	21.9	27.8	31.4	50.5	66.5
1990–91	21.2	25.5	28.8	35.5	37.8
change (%)	−0.7	−2.3	−2.6	−15.0	−28.7
Real net earnings (% rise)	34.7	37.8	38.5	73.8	140.1
Gross earnings (£ a week) in 1990–91	202.53	303.80	607.60	1519.00	3038.00
Tax + NIC cut in £	1.42	6.99	15.80	227.85	871.91

	Taxpayers (m)	Reduction in tax	
		Total (£m)	£ a head
Range of individual's income in 1990–91 (£)			
Under 5,000	2.9	480	110
5,000–10,000	8.6	2,840	320
10,000–15,000	6.4	4,390	690
15,000–20,000	3.8	3,860	1,030
20,000–30,000	2.6	4,190	1,590
30,000–50,000	1.0	3,300	3,270
50,000–70,000	0.2	2,160	9,390
Over 70,000	0.2	5,770	36,060

Public Expenditure

Another Thatcherite article of faith was an assault on public spending. As a White Paper of 1979 put it: *Public expenditure is at the heart of Britain's present difficulties.*

The White Paper of March 1980 set a target of reducing it by 4% in 1983/4 over 1979/80. In the event it *rose* by 6.3%. This was partly explained by the recession and the rise in unemployment, but there was also an increase in spending on law and order and defence, about which Thatcher would be sanguine, and there were overshoots by the local authorities, about which she definitely would not be sanguine.

I SUCCEEDED IN CUTTING BACK EXPENDITURE ON HOUSING AND EDUCATION.

AND, ONCE THE ECONOMY STARTED GROWING, THE PUBLIC SPENDING SHARE OF NATIONAL INCOME FELL –

FROM 46.8% IN 1982/3 TO UNDER 40% BY THE LATE 1980s, THE LOWEST LEVEL FOR TWENTY YEARS.

Public expenditure was not the only area where reality differed from the rhetoric. Thatcher could be charged with inconsistency in her views on the economy, and especially on the level of the £. In 1985 as the £ sank towards parity with the $ she demanded of Chancellor Lawson why sterling was not already in the ERM (exchange rate mechanism) and "protected from all this". Three years later she was hostile to joining the ERM and announcing to the Commons, "There is no way in which you can buck the market."

Some thought that the new enterprise culture of lower taxes and less restriction had brought great improvement. In May 1988 in a *Fortune* article entitled "Britain is Back", John Banham of the Confederation of British Industry claimed: "There's a new generation over here. They're hungry and they like winning."

Others were not so sure, and criticized the devastation wrought on British industry in Thatcher's first administration. A House of Lords Select Committee, which included leading businessmen and prominent scientists, reported in 1987: *Ultimately the goal is the UK's survival as a leading industrial nation in world competition. The UK must therefore spend sufficiently to improve, or at least maintain, its industrial and cultural base relative to those countries which are judged to be its natural competitors . . . Neither government nor industry is spending enough at present levels to restore our industrial position in world markets.*

Monetarism

As the Thatcherites had preached monetary control more strongly than almost any other economic dogma, we should perhaps judge their success by looking at their achievement in this area.

"Monetarism" and "monetarist" came to be used pejoratively to describe what people, usually critics, thought of as "Thatcherism" and "Thatcherite". Strictly speaking, it is the recognition of the importance of money and money supply in an economy.

Keynes would undoubtedly have adapted his views to cope with the economic conditions of the 1960s and 70s which were different from those of the 1920s and 30s when he wrote his most influential works, culminating in *The General Theory of Employment, Interest and Money* (1936).

Nevertheless, Keynes did believe that governments had a role in ensuring sufficient demand in the economy to maintain full employment. Keynesians also believed in involving the big players – the "social actors" – the employers' organization, the CBI (Confederation of British Industry), and the workers' organization, the TUC (Trades Union Congress) in the managing of the economy.

The structural weakness of the British economy, with its slowness in adapting from the old basic industries of coal, steel, shipbuilding and chemicals to the modern growth ones of electronics, computers and telecommunications, allied to weak management, myopic trade unions and inept government, led to recurring financial crises so that by the mid 1970s the whole Keynesian consensus approach was discredited.

Denis Healey, Labour Chancellor of the Exchequer 1974–79, initially tried to cope with the high inflation and low growth exacerbated by the oil crisis of the mid 1970s with the usual Keynesian weapons, including a so-called "Social Contract" with the unions.

To a certain extent, a new approach closer to the monetarism to be more rigorously pursued by the first Thatcher administration was imposed by the IMF, and Prime Minister James Callaghan, with one eye on the financial markets, told the Labour Party Conference in September 1976: *We used to think that you could spend your way out of a recession and increase employment by cutting taxes and increasing government spending. I tell you in all candour that that option no longer exists, and that insofar as it ever did exist, it only worked on each occasion since the War by injecting a bigger dose of inflation into the economy, followed by a higher level of unemployment as the next step.*

But Callaghan and Healey were not really pursuing a true monetarist approach in the late 1970s. They still used incomes policies, there was no medium-term financial plan or framework, and once the crisis had passed, plans for increasing government spending were wheeled out again.

In contrast, prompted by Keith Joseph, there was an ideological commitment in the Thatcher faction of the Tory Party to pursue a monetarist approach.

In Britain, academic support was given by the Money Study Group as well as the IEA and CPS.

The most significant of the monetarist academics, apart from Alan Walters, were **Brian Griffiths** (b. 1941), Professor of Economics at the City University, and later Head of the Prime Minister's Policy Unit, and **Patrick Minford** (b. 1943), Professor of Applied Economics at Liverpool University. There were also some City economists banging the monetarist drum, most notably **Tim Congdon** (b. 1949) and **Gordon Pepper** (b. 1934). By the time Thatcher came to power in 1979, anyone who had been following the economic debate at all should have been prepared for an experiment in monetarism.

The launching of Thatcher's monetarism is often credited to Keith Joseph's speech in Preston in September 1974 when he said,

The monetarist thesis has been caricatured as implying that if we get the flow of money spending right everything will be right. This is not – repeat not – my belief. What I believe is that if we get the money supply wrong – too high or too low – nothing will come right. Monetary control is a pre-essential for everything else we need and want to do; an opportunity to tackle the real problems – labour shortage in one place, unemployment in another; exaggerated expectations; inefficiencies, frictions and distortions; hard-core unemployment.

The truth is that, in power, Thatcher abandoned monetary targets. Ian Gilmour, one of the early sackings from Thatcher's cabinet, referred to monetarism as "the uncontrollable in pursuit of the indefinable". In the early 1980s monetary targets were retained but were constantly revised upwards.

Monetary growth: per cent annual rate of increase

	Target	Actual
1979–80	7–11	12.0
1980–1	7–11	19.0
1081–2	6–10	13.0
1982–3	8–12	11.0
1983–4	7–11	10.0
1984–5	6–10	13.5
1985–6	5–9	15.3
1986–7	11–15	20.0

As growth and its benefits were appreciated by the electorate, the attitude to inflation was eased and the official stance modified from eradication to "downward pressure". After 1985, monetary targets were virtually abandoned and in 1986 when the price of oil fell sharply, Chancellor Lawson opted for a falling value of the £ and growth rather than keeping up the war on inflation.

In the early days of Thatcher's first administration, many thought "Thatcherism = Monetarism, Full Stop". No one held this simplistic view by her third administration. Indeed, monetarism had been virtually abandoned, almost discredited. John Major, Chief Secretary to the Treasury, June 1987–June 1989, and Chancellor, October 1989–November 1990, told the Treasury and Civil Service Committee in 1989 . . .

Academics David Butler and Dennis Kavanagh said: *Despite pockets of impoverishment, Britain was turning into an ever more middle-class society.*

But for the poor, life became even worse. Although the level of supplementary benefit increased slightly in real terms until it was replaced in the 1988 reorganization of social security, its upgrading lagged well behind the rise in earnings. In 1978 it was 61% of average personal disposable income, by 1987 it was only 53%.

The Family Expenditures Survey showed that the real incomes of the bottom 10% *fell* by 9.7% between 1979 and 1985. By the late 1980s over 8 million people were dependent on income support, with a hard core of over 1.5 million drawing benefit for more than 5 years.

To exacerbate the situation, the Thatcher government froze child benefit after April 1987. The Child Poverty Action Group said that the Thatcher government brought horizontal distribution between poor and poor rather than vertical redistribution from rich to poor.

HOMELESS FAMILIES ROSE FROM 50,000 TO 120,000 (REPRESENTING 370,000 PEOPLE).

BY THE MID 1980s, SOME THOUGHTFUL TORIES WERE EXPRESSING DOUBTS ABOUT THATCHERITE POLICIES.

THE FRUITS OF ECONOMIC SUCCESS COULD TURN SOUR UNLESS WE CAN BRING BACK SOCIAL COHESION TO OUR COUNTRY.

Douglas Hurd, Home Secretary

The Economist began by supporting Edward Heath in the Conservative leadership election of 1975 in which Thatcher defeated him. By 1987 it was saying what every travelling Briton had come to know: *. . . the dispiriting sense of crossing the Channel or the Atlantic to find cleaner streets, fuller shops, snappier clothes and smarter hospitals . . .*

For years, many Britons consoled themselves with the thought that . . . they could still ensure a genteel life in the second league. Only when the third league – the Singapores, South Koreas and Brazils – began pinching chunks of British business did people start to realise that comfortable inertia was not an option. The choice was either to compete or to decline in growing discomfort.

In *The Economist*'s view, the choice, thanks to Thatcher, had been made. In the five years 1982–6, Britain's GDP had grown by 14.5%, France's by 8% and West Germany's by 9%. "The sliding has stopped."

According to Thatcher's Chief Press Secretary, **Bernard Ingham** (b. 1932), it was Thatcher's refusal to accept this inexorable decline that stands as her greatest achievement. In his book, *Kill the Messenger,* he said . . .

Even the left-wing historian **Eric Hobsbawm** (b. 1917) conceded in his book, *Age of Extremes*: *Even the British Left was eventually to admit that some of the ruthless shocks imposed on the British economy by Mrs Thatcher had probably been necessary. There were good grounds for some of the disillusion with state-managed industries and public administration that became so common in the 1980s.*

Thatcher herself put it this way when she told *The Times* in February 1984 . . .

I CAME TO OFFICE WITH ONE DELIBERATE INTENT, TO CHANGE BRITAIN FROM A DEPENDENT TO A SELF-RELIANT SOCIETY - FROM A GIVE-IT-TO-ME TO A DO-IT-YOURSELF NATION; TO A GET-UP-AND-GO INSTEAD OF A SIT-BACK-AND-WAIT BRITAIN.

The *Guardian* journalist, Hugo Young, in his book *One of Us,* also conceded that some of Thatcher's economic achievements were considerable: *In the estimation of the world, Britain was now among the strong economies. Productivity, in particular, was dramatically higher than a decade before . . . The overmanning was a thing of the past . . . Some of the policies which contributed were distinctive Thatcherite policies, and were remarkably successful. Prime place was almost universally accorded to the remorseless shrinking of trade union power.*

The Thatcher Style

Modern democracies are very difficult to govern to the satisfaction of the electorate. One of the main problems for incoming governments is the necessity to promise far more than they can ever hope to deliver.

Thatcher was more determined than most. Ivor Crewe, Professor of Government, writing on Thatcher values, said: *She has firm convictions on almost every issue under the sun. Not since Gladstone has Britain been led by such an opinionated and evangelical Prime Minister. Most Prime Ministers see themselves as "healers" (for example, John Major wanted to make Britain a nation "at ease with itself"); a few, like Lloyd George and Churchill, as warriors; Thatcher, uniquely, saw herself as a crusader.*

Robert (now **Lord**) **Skidelsky** (b. 1939), biographer of Keynes and no right-winger, said of Thatcher that she was a warrior in the mould of Boadicea, Elizabeth the First and Florence Nightingale, both physically and morally brave, and that she was: *The most ideological Prime Minister to have led a party which prided itself on its pragmatism. She got her chance because the old pragmatism had degenerated into a sticky corporatism which had become the vehicle for stagnation and decline.*

Skidelsky admired her courage but he was more critical of her approach to human relations, feeling that she found it impossible to win friends by arguments or to conciliate former enemies.

Julian Critchley (b. 1930), a Tory MP never promoted, made the memorable remark: *She cannot see an institution without hitting it with her handbag.*

If this style was appropriate in the early days of her government, it became increasingly counter-productive, so that by the late 1980s all but her closest supporters had tired of it.

Many, especially those condemned by Thatcher as "wets", thought that the Thatcherite tone, whatever the substance, was damaging. **Francis Pym** (b. 1922), sacked by Thatcher in 1983, said: *I think that the public tone of the government has often sounded unsympathetic . . . Conviction, determination and forceful logic can easily turn into dogmatism, inflexibility and insensitivity. As a result, people feel that the government neither understands nor cares about them. This causes immense harm.*

Anthony King, Professor of Government, described what he called "fear at first hand": *She puts the fear of God into people.*

Joe Rogaly of the *Financial Times* wrote that Britain had been *governed by a Prime Minister who, whatever her faults, has been infused with a vision. She has been a driven woman, always urging ministers forward, terrifying them, tiring them out one by one, disposing of them, nagging them, politicising their senior officials, popping in on this or that issue, scrawling her comments on everything, vetoing this, insisting on that, overshadowing all.*

Christopher Johnson in *The Economy Under Mrs Thatcher* described her style as similar to de Gaulle's: "It was *le gouvernement par la parole*, government by public pronouncement. De Gaulle used his press conferences at the Elysée Palace to make policy; Mrs Thatcher used *The Jimmy Young Show*."

Not Ideas But Action

Even one of her greatest supporters, Lord Harris, did not think of Thatcher as a creator of original ideas: *She doesn't have an original idea in her head.* But he still admired her: *That's not meant to be offensive: politicians aren't meant to have original ideas. But she has some instincts. And she brought to that superhuman courage that daily withstood the assault that was almost unremitting through the whole of the 1980s.*

And Enoch Powell, who ought to have admired her, was also dismissive of her ability to cope with ideas.

Alfred Sherman said: *Mrs T never "thunk" any thoughts. She took other people's ideas.*

Thatcherism began less as a doctrine than as a mood. From the outset, the beliefs and values that underlie Thatcherism have been more identifiable than its ideas . . . The mood that Thatcher seized and rode to power reflected not only a general disillusionment with the bipartisan post-war settlement but also with the hypocrisy of socialism and its self-seeking proletarian cant. (Alfred Sherman)

Thatcher made clear her contempt for teachers and academics and her preference for men of action: *And nowhere is this attitude of opposition to wealth creation more marked than in the cloister and the common room. What these critics apparently can't stomach is that wealth creators have a tendency to acquire wealth in the process of creating it for others. They didn't speak with Oxford accents. They hadn't got what people call "the right connections"; they had just one thing in common. They were men of action.*

Amongst her men of action, several were Jews. No other cabinet has had so many. Harold Macmillan quipped: "There are more old Estonians than old Etonians." One of her favourites was **David Young** (b. 1932), whom she elevated to the peerage in 1984 so that she could have him in the cabinet.

Norman Strauss said: *She reaches for Jewish people because they do partly personify the Thatcherite virtues. They are entrepreneurial. They are successful people anywhere. They believe in family life . . . They believe in thrift and savings and doing things by your own efforts: in self-help.*

John Biffen added: *It is difficult to talk about this: it puts people in a great tizz. But it just happens that the intellectual thrust of the new liberal economics substantially came from the Jewish intellectual élite. The Jews she had in government were all very much of the new radical Right.*

And if Thatcherites did not believe, in theory, in solving everyone's problems by government action, Thatcher did believe in shaking up the Establishment – the civil service, heads of nationalized industries, bankers, academics, doctors, barristers, the BBC, local authorities and unions – who, in her opinion, were responsible for denigrating the vigorous virtues or holding them in check.

Thatcher herself could be very simplistic, not to say populist, when she was extolling her own virtues. She told the *News of the World* in 1981 . . .

And if Thatcher could be simplistic, according to John Biffen, she "was instinctive and sometimes quite bewildering in the pursuit of economic policy. She welcomed a free exchange rate provided it never floated downwards; she despised subsidies but fought like a tigress to protect mortgage interest rate relief."

Authoritarian

Thatcher had talked in a speech at the Tory Party Conference as early as 1986 of there being too much government.

WHAT WE NEED IS A FAR GREATER DEGREE OF PERSONAL RESPONSIBILITY AND DECISION, FAR MORE INDEPENDENCE FROM THE GOVERNMENT, AND A COMPARATIVE REDUCTION IN THE ROLE OF GOVERNMENT.

However, in office, she seemed unable to resist the temptation to tell everyone what to do and, where it was in the considerable power enjoyed by a Prime Minister, to make sure they did.

Many were concerned about the attacks on civil liberty by what they saw as an authoritarian and autocratic government. The *New Statesman and Society* magazine launched "Charter 88", arguing that: *The government has eroded a number of important civil freedoms: the universal right to habeas corpus, to peaceful assembly, to freedom of information, to freedom of expression, to membership of a trade union, to local government, to freedom of movement . . . By taking these rights from some, the government puts them at risk for all.*

Thatcher only confirmed people's view that she was both authoritarian and autocratic.

Will Hutton (b. 1950), a *Guardian* journalist during Thatcher's reign and later editor of *The Observer* and author of the best-selling book, *The State We're In,* felt that she became a virtual dictator, filling every conceivable post with her supporters.

As the final leadership contest unfolded, the *Sunday Times* wrote: *The crisis is entirely the responsibility of the Prime Minister, of her arrogance, of the contempt with which she treats her colleagues . . . she will destroy any minister who crosses her, she lacks the common sense and even . . . the common decency to preside over a talented cabinet; she has become a menace to our system of government.*

Conclusion

Who is correct? The Conservative historian, Lord Blake, who wrote in *The Times* on the occasion of Thatcher's resignation: *Margaret Thatcher's place in history is assured; the first woman to be Prime Minister, the first since Palmerston to win three successive General Elections, the longest continuous holder of the office since Lord Liverpool . . . She was on the British political scene a giant among pygmies. She was one of the two greatest Prime Ministers in the 20th century and one of the half dozen greatest Prime Ministers of all parties and all times.*

Or Will Hutton, editor of *The Observer*? *Her actual achievement was modest, even destructive, for in economic and political terms she did no more than entrench the vicious circles in which the country is trapped. She was only able to mask the full implications temporarily with a credit boom.*

The answer is probably somewhere between these two extreme views. But on one institution, she did have a marked effect.

Thatcher's Influence on New Labour

There was no doubt that Labour must change if they ever wanted to return to power. Clause 4 and the social reforms of Sidney and Beatrice Webb really were from a former age. Even the union victories of the 1970s were a long time ago. The 1990s were for the young, aspiring middle class. When the Labour Party issued its policy document, *Looking to the Future,* on 4 May 1990, *The Times,* owned by Thatcher supporter, Rupert Murdoch, said . . .

Out went:

commitment to re-nationalization

government controls over the economy and industry

taxes to enforce repatriation of capital overseas

repeal of all Conservative trade union reforms.

Not quite out but reduced to near invisibility was: support for nuclear disarmament.

The Times concluded that the document was "a retreat not just from some naive socialism" – socialism was reduced to "dust on the shelf".

Labour now proclaimed its belief in the market and disclaimed an "irresponsible dash for growth". In industrial relations, almost all Conservative reforms were accepted, including the end of the closed shop, ballots on strikes and union elections. There was no mention of those 1970s recipes (of both Tory and Labour governments) – controls on incomes, prices and foreign exchange. The sale of council houses was accepted.

Barrister, novelist and Labour supporter **John Mortimer** (b. 1923) was horrified by the "new" Labour Party: *The present creed of the Labour Party, should it exist, is only hidden under a number of businesslike breasts wearing dark blue suits and anonymous, but not quite regimental, ties.*

And Hugo Young wrote in *The Guardian* in July 1990: *Market economics and fiscal rigour are now agreed by the centre-left to be the cornerstones of any policy practical people can agree on.*

By 1996, the Labour Party entertained high hopes of winning power in the coming Election, and its young leader, Tony Blair, openly expressed admiration for the determination of Thatcher. His party, led by what was termed "New Labour", not only wanted to retain Trident, the nuclear deterrent, but said it would press the button if necessary. It would reform comprehensives and leave the grammar schools alone. It erected new limits around state intervention in the market and even announced it would spend less rather than more on welfare benefits. You don't come much more Thatcherite than that.

Jonathan Powell, Blair's chief of staff, declared: "Thatcher is his model."

The Appeal of Thatcherism Elsewhere in the World

It is not only the British Labour Party that has taken what it sees as the best of Thatcherism on board. Countries throughout the world, especially, and perhaps ironically, in former Eastern Europe, but also in Mexico, Brazil and the Far East, have adopted many Thatcherite governmental methods, particularly privatization.

As *The Economist* said in March 1995: *Privatization has become the political creed of the 1990s. Governments of every stripe from Moscow to Mexico City are selling their state-owned firms as fast as they can. Privatization has even caught on in the United States.*

In both 1994 and 1995, nationalized firms worth over $60 billion were privatized worldwide.

The Lasting Effects of Thatcher

Thatcherism is British and for Britain. It is not an *ism* like "Marxism" or "Libertarianism" or even "Feminism", designed to embrace like-minded people across the world. It can be picked up by another nation state and applied to itself, but it is not an international idea as such.

As time puts perspective on the Thatcher years, it is already safe to say that there was . . .

A Thatcher Era

and that there has come into being something called . . .

Thatcherism

In looking at the *Thatcher Era,* we only have to think, was there a Callaghan era, a Heath era, a Wilson era? to see that it holds true.

Britain went into it . . .

a dispirited, second (or was it third?) division, overmanned, union-bullied, under-managed, poorly performing, bureaucratized, inefficient, subsidized, benefit-demanding, class-ridden society living with the comforting certainties of the Cold War

and came out of it . . .

a lively, definitely second division, relatively lean, union-cowed, well-managed, reasonably performing, not-quite-so-bureaucratized, less inefficient, still hopelessly subsidized and benefit-demanding, class-ridden society facing the uncertain realities of freed Communist states, most of whom quickly adopted Thatcherite practice.

"Thatcherism" has been dubbed as symbolizing greed, the triumph of the strong over the weak, materialism, little England and a world peopled only by philistines.

Others might see it as a creed which . . .

rewards effort

confronts bullies

faces up to difficult issues

realizes the strength of world competition

and stands up for what is right, not what is easy.

A major criticism of Thatcherism was its failure to establish an independent Bank of England which could, like the Federal Reserve Board in the USA and the Bundesbank in Germany, provide a strong bulwark against any future revival of inflation. Alex Brummer, City editor of *The Guardian,* writing immediately after Thatcher's resignation, supported an independent Bank of England: *Such a move . . . would provide reassurance on commitment to sound money while having the flexibility to use fiscal policy to do those things necessary to undo the wrongs of Thatcherism, which produced private prosperity but at a high cost of public squalor and financial hooliganism.*

Further Reading

In a sense it is too soon to write **Thatcher for Beginners** because the consequences of Thatcher's period in office have not yet been fully played out. We debated for nearly five years whether we should write and publish the book, and came to the conclusion in early 1996 that there *is* such a thing as Thatcherism, though it means different things to people, and that there *was* an era constantly referred to as the "Thatcherite era". To many, the eighties was Thatcher and vice versa. She is already important and significant, and will probably become more so.

There will be many more books written on Thatcher, Thatcherism and the eighties, but here is some suggested reading which is already available:

One of Us, Hugo Young (Macmillan 1990)
Hugo Young, the well-known *Guardian* journalist, has written the most comprehensive biography of Thatcher. As a leading political journalist throughout the 1970s and 80s, he was very close to all the leading politicians of the day.

The Thatcher Era, Peter Riddell (Basil Blackwell 1991)
Alongside Young, Peter Riddell has been another acute political observer and journalist of the last 20 years.

Thatcher's People, John Ranelagh (Harper Collins 1991)
John O'Bierne Ranelagh has been an author and television broadcaster for nearly 25 years and knows many of the movers and shakers around Thatcher. He views her sympathetically but realistically.

The Thatcher Effect, Dennis Kavanagh and Anthony Selden (Clarendon Press 1989)
Kavanagh and Selden are two well-known commentators on post-war British history.

Tories and the Welfare State, Timothy Raison (Macmillan 1990)
Timothy Raison was a successful Tory MP from 1970 until 1992 and could therefore comment from close experience on Thatcher's approach to the Welfare State.

The Collected Works of F. A. Hayek, Bruce Caldwell (Routledge 1995)
The Essence of Hayek, Chiaki Nishiyama and Kurt Leube (Hoover Institution Press 1984)
These two books are important if you want to look further into the thoughts and writing of Hayek.

The Economy Under Mrs Thatcher 1979–90, Christopher Johnson (Penguin Books 1991)
Johnson was a journalist with *The Times* and the *Financial Times*, and moved on to become chief economic adviser to Lloyds Bank from 1977 to 1991. This book explodes many Thatcherite claims of success with the economy.

The State We're In, Will Hutton (Jonathan Cape 1995)
This book was a best-seller in 1995 and 1996 and was at one time talked of as New Labour's manifesto for the next election. As Hutton is a strong advocate of increasing public spending, New Labour distanced itself from him for fear of upsetting the City. He did not like Thatcher or her policies, and she would not like his views.

The Anatomy of Thatcherism, Shirley Robin Letwin (Fontana 1992)
In contrast to Hutton, Shirley Letwin was a great fan of Thatcher. She was a director of the Centre for Policy Studies, which was founded by Thatcher and Keith Joseph.

The Politics of Thatcherism, Stuart Hall and Martin Jacques
(Lawrence and Wishart 1983)
This book was published in association with *Marxism Today*, which tells you where it's coming from.

Words as Weapons, Paul Foot (Verso 1990)
Paul Foot specializes in exposing the greed and follies of Tories in high office; nor does he spare the weak Labour opposition of the 1980s.

The Politics and Economics of the Poll Tax, John Gibson (Einas 1990)
Failure in British Government: The Politics of the Poll Tax, David Butler, Andrew Adonis and Tony Travers (Oxford University Press 1994)
These two books will tell you all you need to know about the ill-fated poll tax.

The Rise of the British Presidency, Michael Foley
(Manchester University Press 1993)
This book attempts to portray Thatcher's style of government as presidential.

Taking Stock of Thatcherism, Ulf Hedetoft and Hans Niss
(Aalborg University 1991)
Margaret Thatcher, in Victory and Downfall 1987 and 1990, Bruce Geelhold
(Praeger 1992)
These two books are interesting observations from outside the UK.

Prime Minister, Bernard Donoughue (Jonathan Cape 1987)
Lord Donoughue was a senior policy adviser to Prime Ministers Harold Wilson and Jim Callaghan from 1974 until 1979. He went downhill a little after that, becoming a director of Robert Maxwell's company (a fact not mentioned in his *Who's Who* entry). Nevertheless, he was clearly close to the reins of power in the five years which made it so necessary for the country to have a Prime Minister of Margaret Thatcher's calibre, and for that reason this book should be endured.

Two Decades in British Politics, Bill Jones and Lynton Robins
(Manchester University Press 1992)
A ramble through the 1970s and 80s.

From Boom to Bust, David Smith (Penguin Books 1992)
David Smith is economics editor of the *Sunday Times*, and was a financial journalist throughout the 1980s.

Age of Extremes, Eric Hobsbawm (Michael Joseph 1994)
Hobsbawm is a well-known left-wing historian.

Kill the Messenger, Bernard Ingham (Harper Collins 1991)
Bernard Ingham, as Thatcher's press secretary and, some would say, hatchet-man, lacks objectivity but, like Donoughue, he was close to the source of power.

Below the Parapet, Carol Thatcher (Harper Collins 1996)
Carol Thatcher is, of course, Margaret Thatcher's daughter. The book tells you very little about Thatcher herself, but then it is really a biography of Denis Thatcher.

Biographies

Peter Pugh read history at Cambridge in the mid-1960s before pursuing a business career. His own business died in the first Thatcher administration, his new career – writing corporate histories – prospered in her second and third administrations, and Icon Books, of which he is managing director, was founded in the depths of the recession that followed the Thatcher boom. With that experience he felt qualified to comment, subjectively and, he hopes, objectively, on Thatcher and Thatcherism. He is also the author of *Keynes for Beginners*.

Carl Flint is an eighties throwback, champagne socialist, Islingtonian and neighbour of Tony Blair. He works with cartoon, collage and mixed media, and has been published in everything from *NME* and *Sonic* in the UK to *Comic Morning* in Japan. He also illustrated *Joyce for Beginners*.

Author's Acknowledgements
The *Beginners* series is about icons that endure, whether they are people or -isms. I debated with my partners, Jeremy Cox and Richard Appignanesi, for a number of years as to whether Thatcher and Thatcherism would endure. I am grateful to them for agreeing with me that they will endure, if only to describe an era, an attitude and a type of person, and for allowing me to write the book. As always, Richard Appignanesi put logic, structure and life into the text, and Carl Flint has done his usual masterly job with the illustrations.

Artist's Acknowledgements
Thanks to the following for their bodies and minds: Carol Isherwood, P.P. Roy, Lee Damarell, Thomas Westwood, Jonathan Crossland, Bob Tellick, Martin Isherwood, Oscar Zarate, Stuart Harrison.

Special thanks to Tommy Westwood.